Workbook for

TONAL HARMONY

with an Introduction to Twentieth-Century Music

Second Edition

Workbook for

TONAL HARMONY

with an Introduction to Twentieth-Century Music

Second Edition

Stefan Kostka
The University of Texas at Austin

Dorothy Payne
The University of Connecticut at Storrs

Consulting Editor in Music
ALLAN W. SCHINDLER
Eastman School of Music

McGraw-Hill, Inc.
New York St. Louis San Francisco Auckland Bogotá
Caracas Lisbon London Madrid Mexico Milan
Montreal New Delhi Paris San Juan Singapore
Sydney Tokyo Toronto

WORKBOOK TO ACCOMPANY TONAL HARMONY

Second Edition

8 9 MAL MAL 9 8 7 6 5 4 3

ISBN: 0-07-5570173

CONTENTS

B. Fill in alto and tenor parts in these exercises.

1

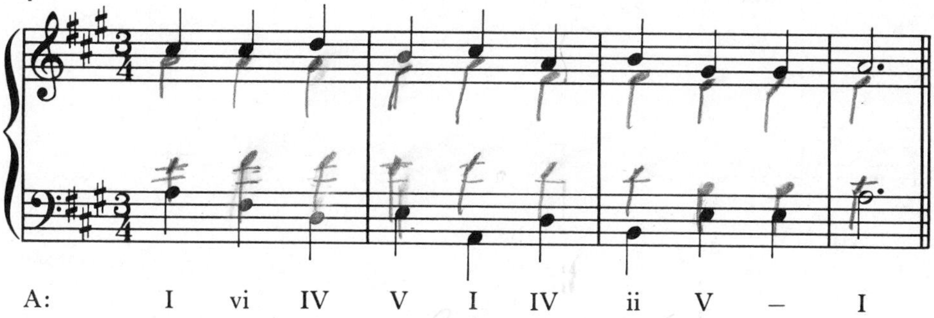

2

3

4

5

d: i IV V i III iv V i VI iv V i

(*not* iv)

C. Add three upper parts to each figured bass to make a four-part choral texture. Review figured bass symbols (pp. 47-49) if necessary. Try to follow all of the spacing and voice-leading conventions discussed in this chapter. Label the chords with roman numerals.

1

2

D. Write the following short progressions in root position for combinations of three and four parts.

1 three parts

E♭: ii V I c♯: i VI iv A: IV V vi

2 four parts

E♭: ii V I c♯: i VI iv A: IV V vi

F: I iii IV D: vi ii V g: VI iv V

EXERCISE 5-8

A. Notate the chords below for the specified instruments. Each chord is written at concert pitch, so transpose as needed for the performers. Use the correct clef for each instrument. Note that the instruments are listed in score order, the order used in Appendix 1, which is not always the same as order by pitch.

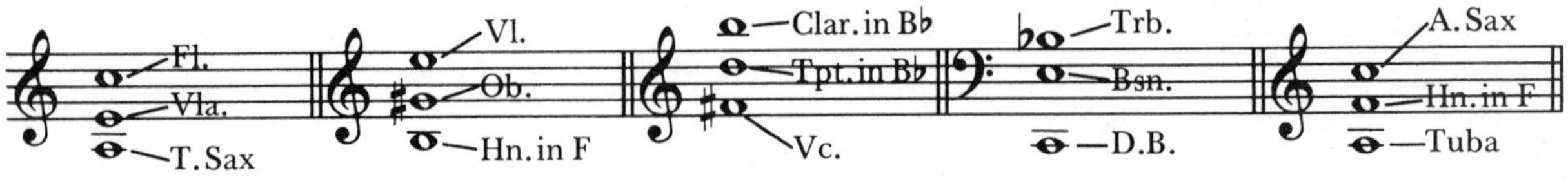

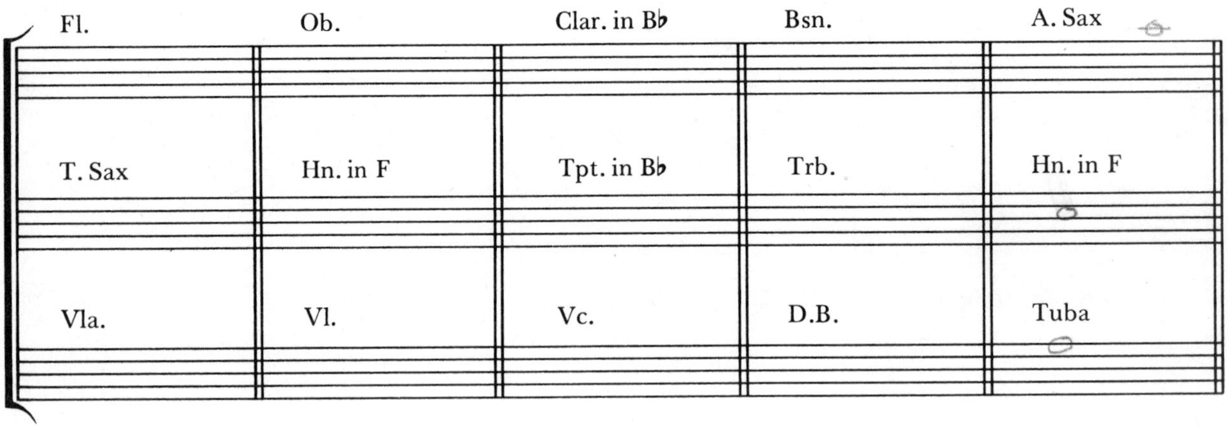

B. Set the following progression for combinations of three and four parts. If possible, score for instruments in your class. Use root position only.

1 three parts (reduced score)

d: i iv V VI iv V i

(full score)

2 four parts (reduced score)

d: i iv V VI iv V i

(full score)

D. Analyze the chords specified by these figured basses, and add inner voices to make a four-part texture. Bracket all circle-of-fifths progressions, even those that contain only two chords.

1

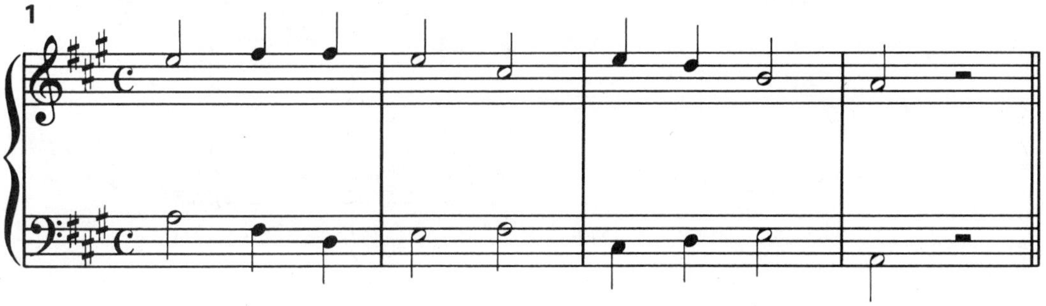

2

3

E. Analyze this figured bass, then add a good soprano line and inner voices. Bracket all circle-of-fifths progressions.

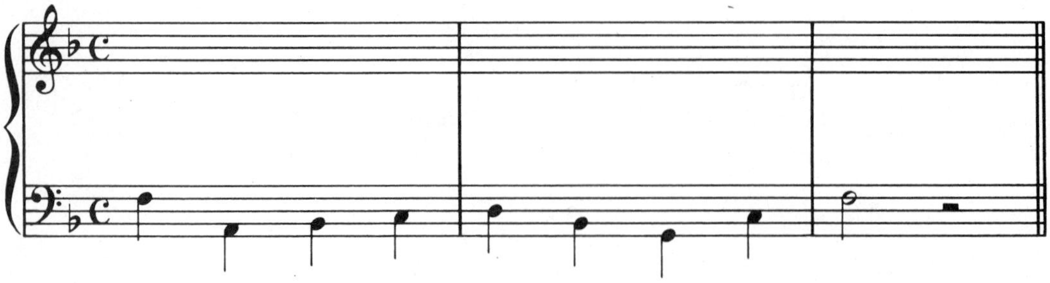

F. Harmonize the melodies below by using root position major or minor (not diminished) triads in an acceptable progression. Try to give the bass a good contour while avoiding parallel and direct 5ths and 8ves with the melody. Be sure to include analysis. Finally, fill in one or two inner parts, as specified by your instructor.

1

G:

2

D:
or b:

2

a:

3

D:

4

e:

J. Select roman numerals with which to harmonize this melody, changing chords every place there is a blank. Be sure your progression is a good one. Then write out the melody with a bass line, using first inversion triads where appropriate. Make sure the bass sounds good when played with the melody and that there are no objectionable parallels. Finally, make a piano setting, using the bass line you composed. Keep the piano texture simple, perhaps like that in Example 7-3 (p. 112).

CHAPTER EIGHT

CADENCES, PHRASES, AND PERIODS

EXERCISE 8-1

A. Cadences. Using only triads in root position and first inversion, make up examples of the following cadences. Each example should include three chords—the two cadence chords plus one chord preceding the cadence chords. Include key signatures and roman numerals.

1 three parts | **2** four parts | **3** three parts | **4** four parts

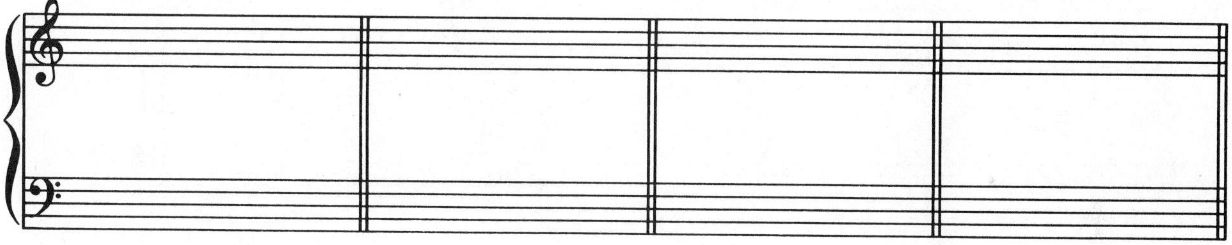

A: ___ ___ ___ (root position IAC)

g: ___ ___ ___ (DC—careful!)

F: ___ ___ ___ (HC)

b: ___ ___ ___ (inverted IAC)

5 three parts | **6** four parts | **7** three parts | **8** four parts

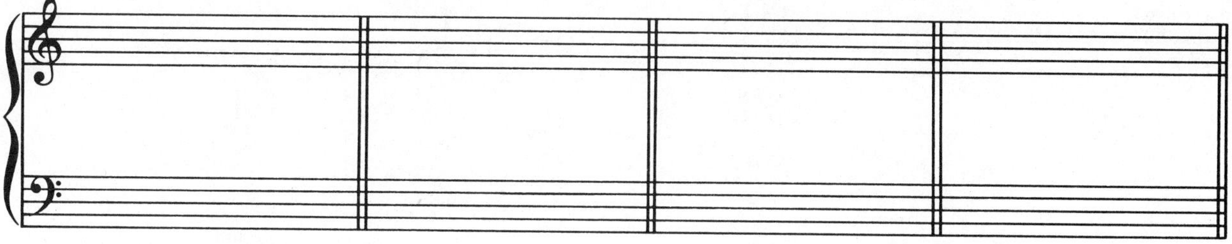

G: ___ ___ ___ (PAC)

d: ___ ___ ___ (PC)

B♭: ___ ___ ___ (leading-tone IAC)

e: ___ ___ ___ (Phrygian HC)

9 three parts **10** four parts **11** three parts **12** four parts

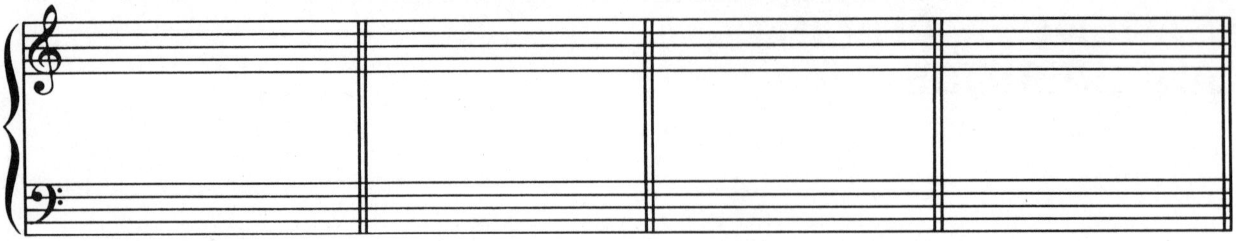

a: ___ ___ ___ (DC—careful!)

C: ___ ___ ___ (PAC)

f: ___ ___ ___ (PC)

D: ___ ___ ___ (HC)

B. Analysis. The cadence chords have been analyzed for you in each example.

1. Make a diagram of this excerpt similar to the diagrams used in the text. Include phrase labels (a, b, and so on), cadence types and measures, and the form of the example.

Schumann, Symphony No. 1, Op. 38, III (piano reduction)

4. This excerpt is in the form of a three-phrase period (some would call it a phrase group). Would it be better to say that it has two antecedent phrases or two consequent phrases? Why? Which phrase features a circle-of-fifths sequence? Analyze all of the chords in that phrase, and diagram the form of the excerpt.

Mozart, Sonata K. 545, I

5. Diagram the form of this excerpt in three ways, all of which are possible interpretations: (1) all four-measure phrases: 4+4+4+4+4; (2) two long phrases plus a short final phrase: 8+8+4; (3) two phrases, the second extended: 8+12. Which interpretation do you prefer? Why?

Mozart, Sonata K. 310, III

6. Diagram the form of this theme, then label the first five chords. Also, see if you can find a disguised sequence hidden in the soprano and another in the bass in mm. 1-8.

Beethoven, Sonata Op. 13, II

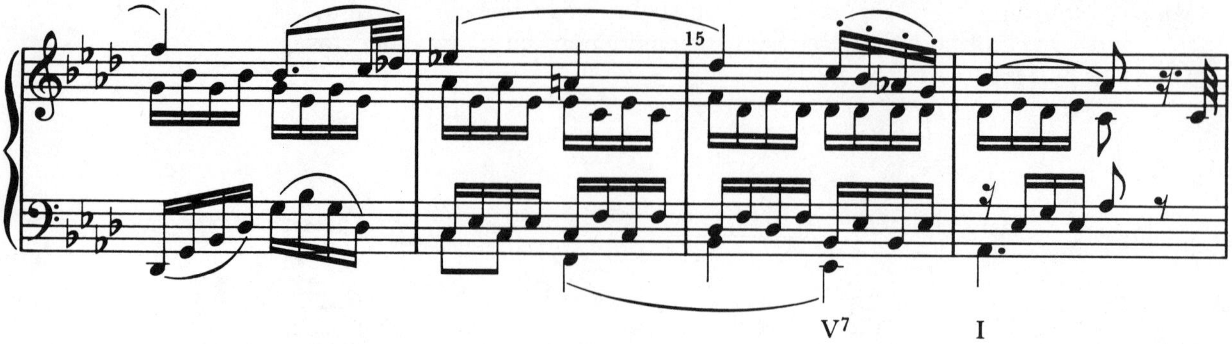

C. Review. Notate the chords in the keys and bass positions indicated.

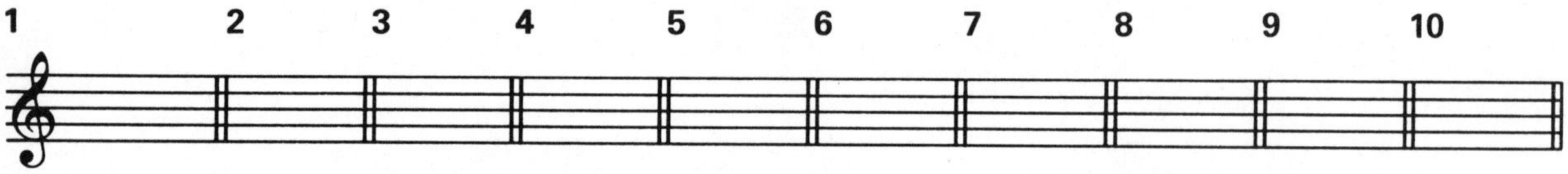

E: I^6 B♭: vi^7 G: IV^6_4 D: ii^4_3 f: VI d: vii^{o6}_5 A♭: iii E♭: $vii^{ø7}$ f♯: V^4_2 A: IV^{M7}

CHAPTER NINE

TRIADS IN SECOND INVERSION

EXERCISE 9-1

A. Analysis. In addition to the specific instructions for each example, label each six-four chord by type.

1. Label all chords with roman numerals.

Schumann, "The Wild Rider," Op. 68, No. 8

2. Label the chords with roman numerals, and put parentheses around all non-chord tones. The bass in m. 87 is E throughout.

Beethoven, Sonata Op. 2, No. 3, III

3. Label chords with roman numerals.

Handel, "Wenn mein Stündlein vorhanden ist"

4. Label chords with roman numerals, and put parentheses around all non-chord tones. Show with brackets the imitation of the soprano part by the bass.

Bach, English Suite No. 2, Courante

B. Fill in one or two inner parts, as specified. Identify any six-four chords by type.

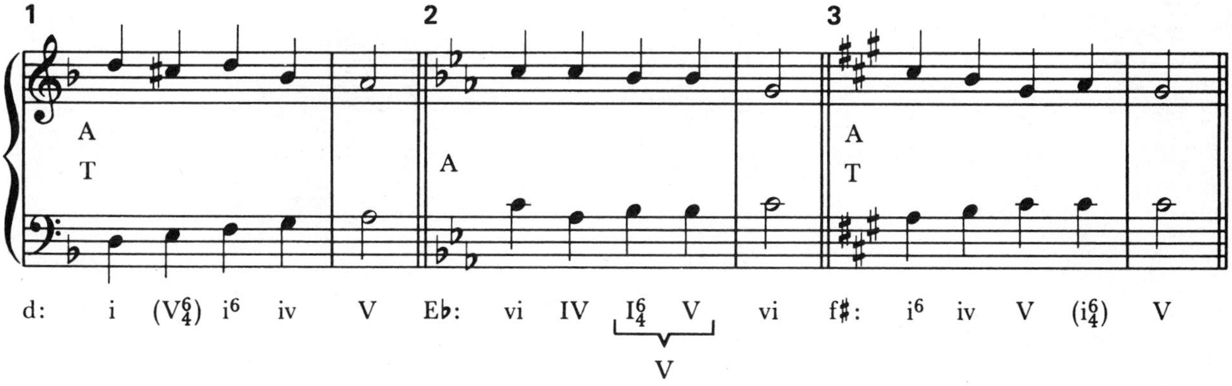

C. Realize these figured basses for three or four voices, as specified. Notice the frequent use of $^{5}_{3}$ (or the equivalent, such as $^{5}_{\sharp}$) to indicate root-position triads following an inverted chord. Analyze with roman numerals and label six-four types.

1

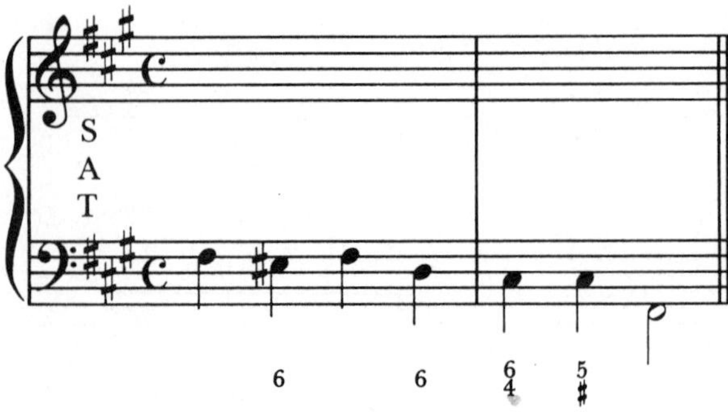

2

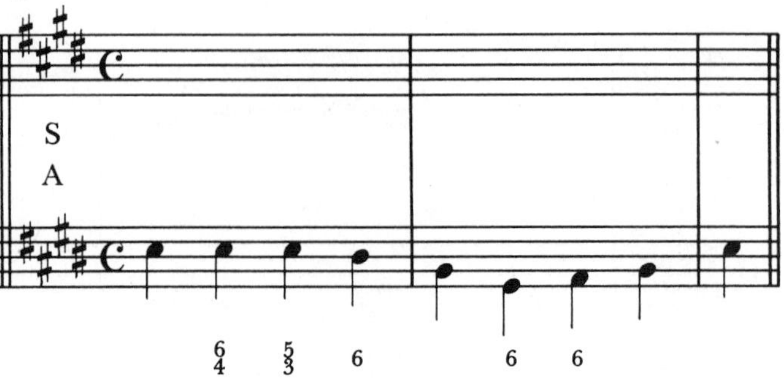

3

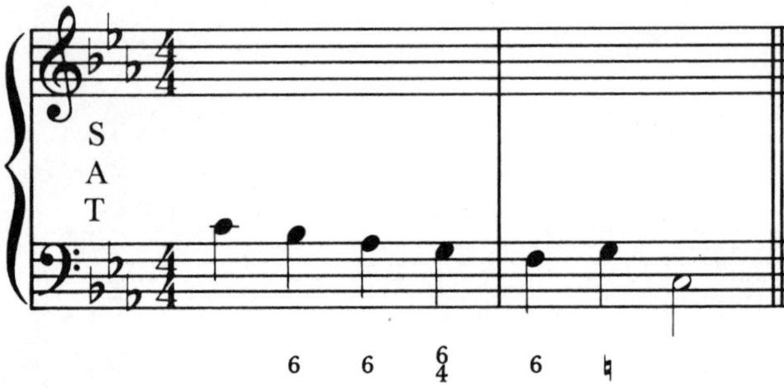

4

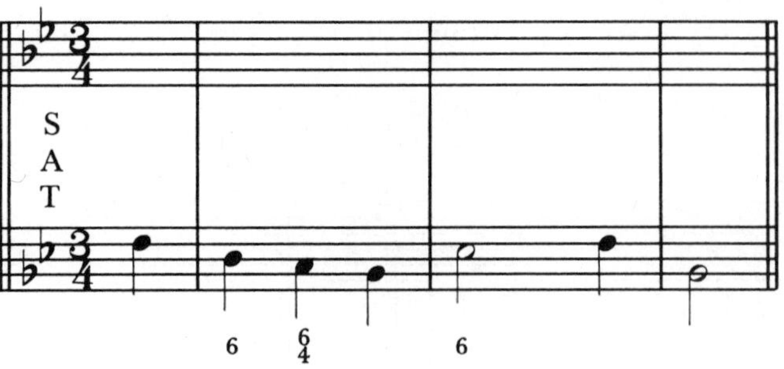

D. Harmonize each unfigured bass with a good tonal progression. Then compose a soprano line that will fit the progression without creating objectionable parallels with the bass. Finally, fill in the specified number of parts to make a four-part texture. Be sure to include a six-four chord in each one.

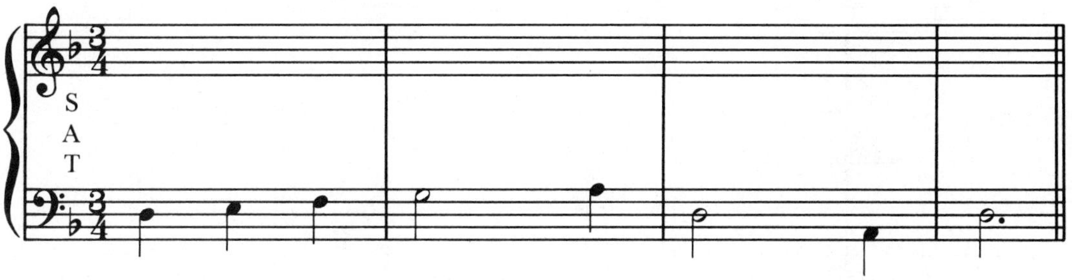

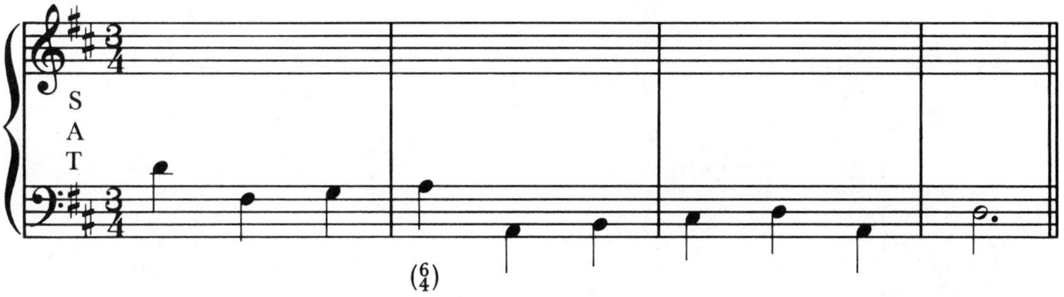

E. Continue the accompaniment of this violin melody. Non-chord tones are in parentheses. Be sure to use at least one cadential, passing, or pedal six-four chord.

CHAPTER TEN

NON-CHORD TONES 1

EXERCISE 10-1

A. Analysis.

1. Go back to Example 5-23 (p. 89), which shows NCTs in parentheses, and identify the type of each NCT in the blanks below. Always show the interval classification (7-6, and so on) when you analyze suspensions.

Alto: ____ ____ ____

Tenor: ____ ____ ____ ____

Bass: ____

2. Analyze the chords and NCTs in this excerpt. Then make a reduction similar to those seen in the text by (1) removing all NCTs, (2) using longer note values or ties for repeated notes, and (3) transposing parts by a P8 where necessary to make the lines smoother. Study the simplified texture. Do any voice-leading problems appear to have been covered up by the embellishments? Discuss the reasons for the leap in the tenor in m. 3.

Bach, "Hilf, Herr Jesu, lass gelingen"

reduction

B. After reviewing pages 171-172, decide what *one* suspension would be best in each excerpt below. Then renotate with the suspension and at least one other embellishment. Remember to put parentheses around NCTs and to label NCTs and arpeggiations.

b: V6 i ii°6 V A: IV6 I V I6 g: i iv i6 vii°6 E♭: IV V6 I V6

C. The example below is a simplified excerpt from a Bach chorale harmonization. Label the chords with roman numerals, and activate the texture with stepwise NCTs. Label all embellishments.

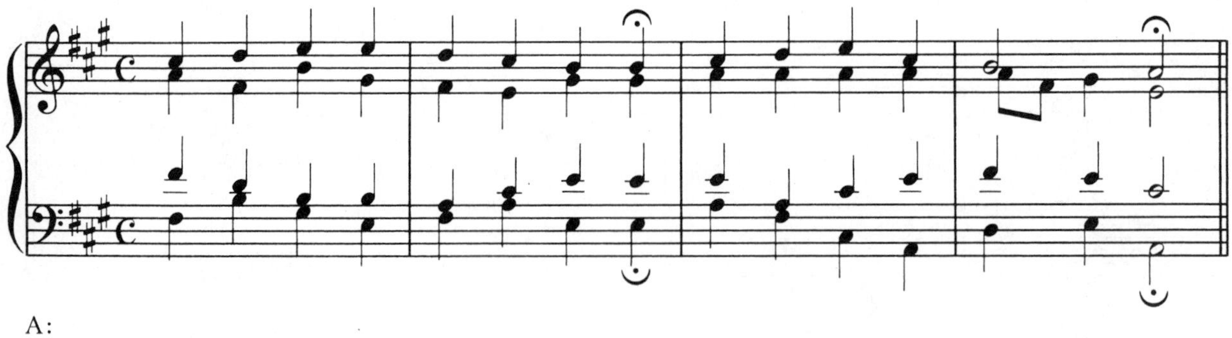

A:

D. Realize these figured basses by analyzing the harmonies, composing a simple melody, and filling in one or two inner parts, as specified. Add some stepwise NCTs to each example. Note: The symbol $^{6-}$ in number 2 calls for a diminished triad with A as the root, with no change of chord above the next C in the bass.

1

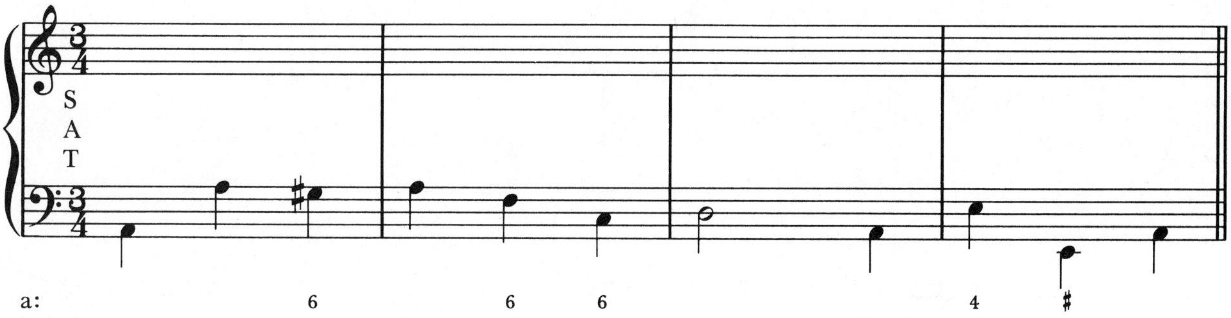

2

E. Using the following progressions, compose a good soprano/bass framework, using inversions where desired. Next add one or two inner parts, as specified. Show with an *x* every possible location for a 9-8, 7-6, 4-3, or 2-3 suspension. Finally, create an elaborated version of the simple texture, including at least one suspension. Other embellishments should be limited to arpeggiations and stepwise NCTs.

1. Three-part texture. (Remember that diminished triads should be used in first inversion.)

2. Four-part texture.

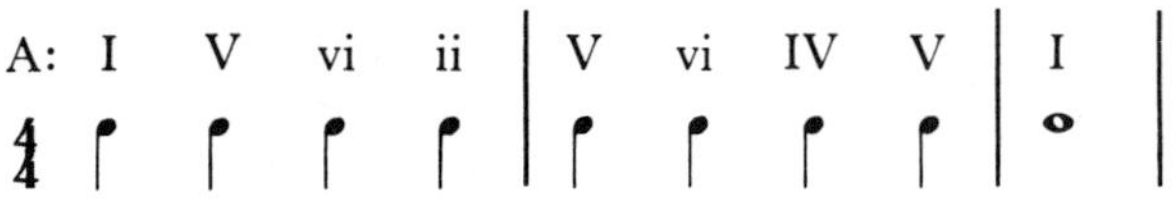

F. Compose your own harmonic progression, and follow the instructions for part E. Try a two-, three-, or four-part texture.

G. Analyze the chords implied by this two-voice framework. Then embellish the framework in an arrangement for string quartet. A suggested beginning is given.

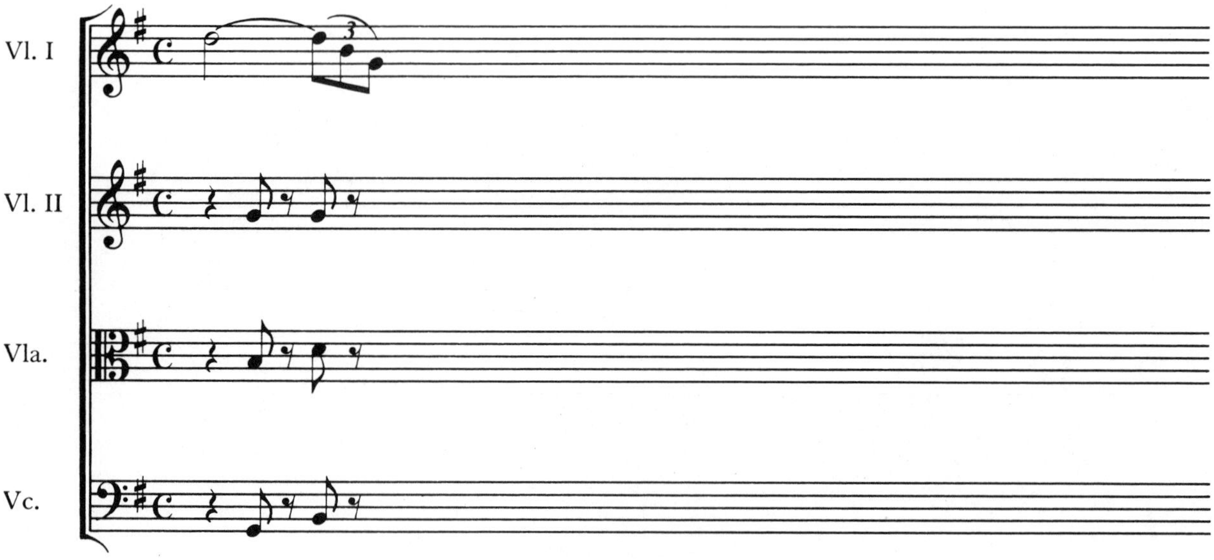

H. Continue your solution to Part G to form a parallel period.

CHAPTER ELEVEN

NON-CHORD TONES 2

EXERCISE 11-1

A. Analysis.

1. Go back to Example 6-16 on page 104 of the text, where NCTs are shown in parentheses, and identify the type of each NCT in the blanks below. Always show the interval classification (7-6, and so on) when you analyze suspensions.

m. 1 ____ ____ m. 3 ____ ____

2. Do the same for Example 8-14 on page 139 of the text.

m. 10 ____ m. 11 ____ m. 13 ____ ____ ____

m. 14 ____ m. 15 ____ m. 16, violin: ____ piano: ____ ____

3. Do the same for Example 9-13 on page 155.

Vl. I: m. 23 ____ m. 24 ____ m. 25 ____ m. 26 ____

Vl. II: m. 23 ____ m. 26 ____ ____ ____

4. Label chords and NCTs in this excerpt.

Schumann, "Roundelay," Op. 68, No. 22

A: ____ ____ ____ ____ ____ ____ V7 ____

5. Label chords and NCTs in this excerpt. Then diagram and label the form.

Mozart, *Eine kleine Nachtmusik,* K. 525, II

6. Label the chords and NCTs, but do not include the pitches called for by the turns (in measures 1 and 3). Bracket any melodic sequences you find.

Beethoven, Sonata Op. 10, No. 1, II

B. Using a three-part texture, write authentic cadences in five different keys, employing a different NCT from the following list in each cadence: p, n, ant, app, e.

C. Compose a simple melody for each figured bass below, and fill in inner voices to make a four-part texture. Include some of the NCTs studied in this chapter. Analyze chords and NCTs.

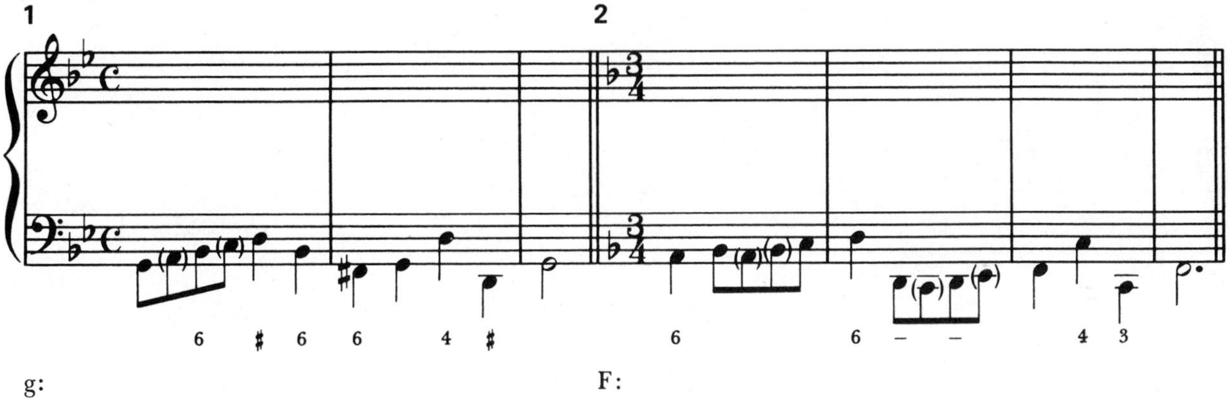

D. Compose a passage in four parts in the key of b minor employing a 7-6 suspension near the beginning and a tonic pedal near the end.

E. Compose eight measures to continue Part A, number 6, on page 76 of this Workbook. Maintain a similar texture, and end with a PAC. Include an NCT studied in this chapter.

F. The framework below is a simplied version of a passage from Mozart's *Magic Flute.* Embellish the framework, turning it into a vocal part (to be sung on neutral syllables) with piano accompaniment.

G. Continue your solution to Part F to form a parallel period.

PART THREE: DIATONIC SEVENTH CHORDS

CHAPTER TWELVE

THE V⁷ CHORD

EXERCISE 12-1

A. The note given in each case is the root, 3rd, 5th, or 7th of a V^7 chord. Notate the chord in root position, and name the major key in which it would be the V^7.

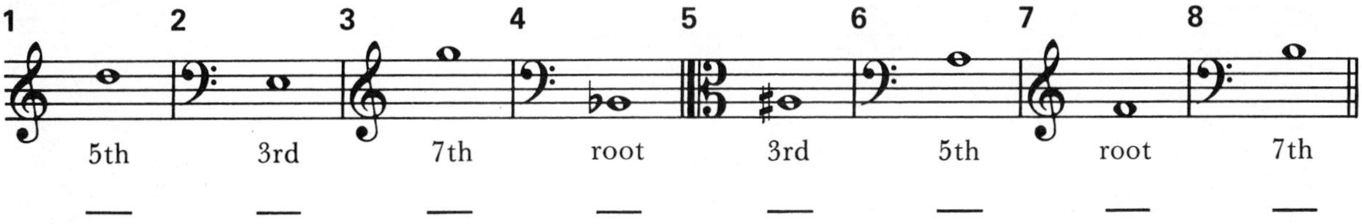

B. Analyze chords and NCTs in the excerpt below. Then discuss the voice leading in the two V^7 chords. (Note: You may have analyzed the B's in the V chords as passing tones, but consider them to be chord 7ths for the purposes of your discussion.)

Bach, "Wir Christenleut'"

C. Resolve each chord to a root position I. (Note: *c* means complete chord, *i* means incomplete chord.)

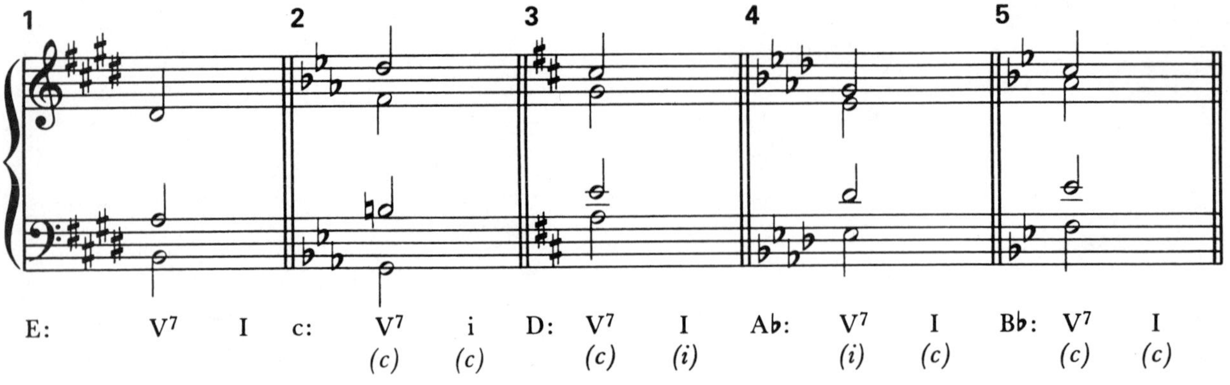

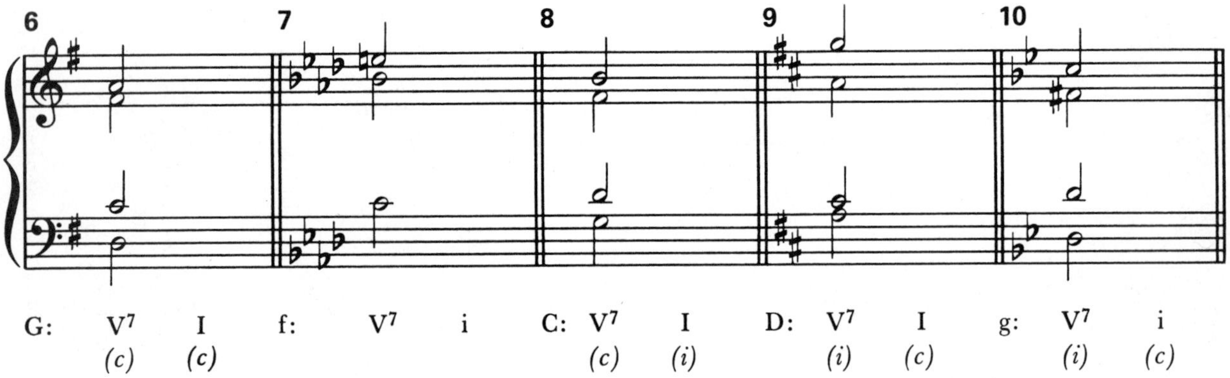

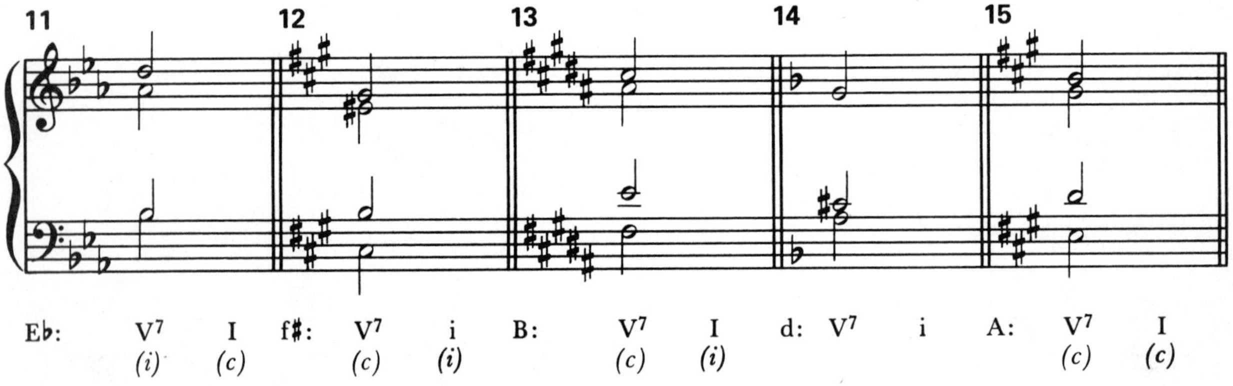

D. Notate the key signature and the V^7 chord, and then resolve it.

1 three parts **2** three parts **3** four parts **4** four parts **5** four parts

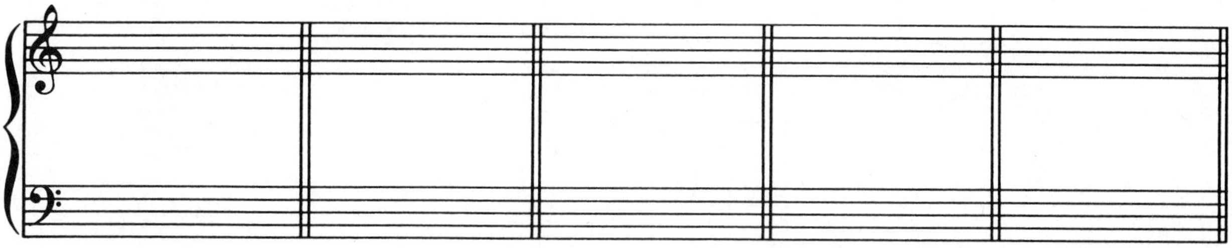

G: V^7 I	d: V^7 i	E: V^7 *(c)* I *(i)*	A♭: V^7 *(c)* I *(c)*	f♯: V^7 *(i)* i *(c)*

6 three parts **7** three parts **8** four parts **9** four parts **10** four parts

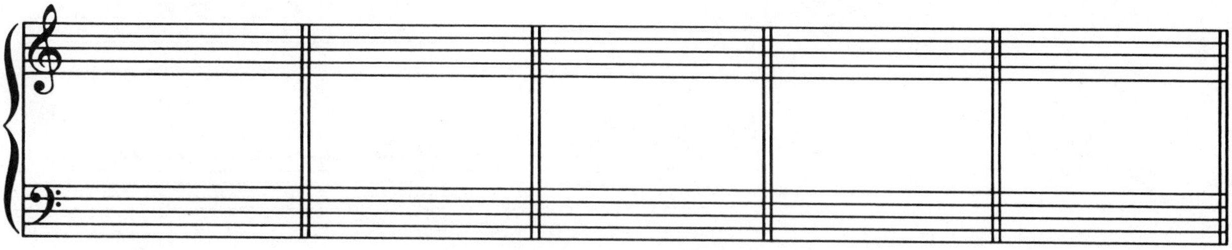

E♭: V^7 vi	A: V^7 vi	f: V^7 VI	b♭: V^7 VI	D: V^7 vi

E. Analyze the harmonies implied by these soprano/bass frameworks. Then make four-part versions with embellishments and at least one root position V^7 chord.

1

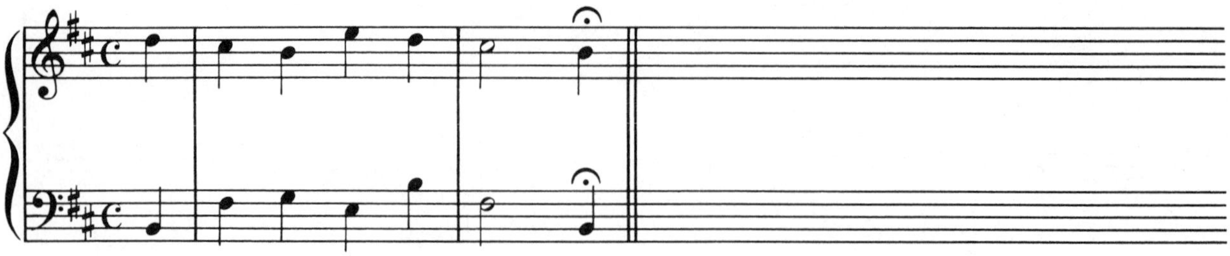

2

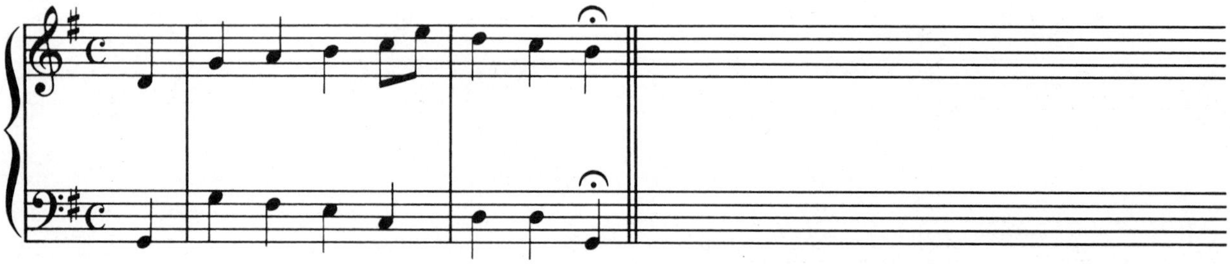

3

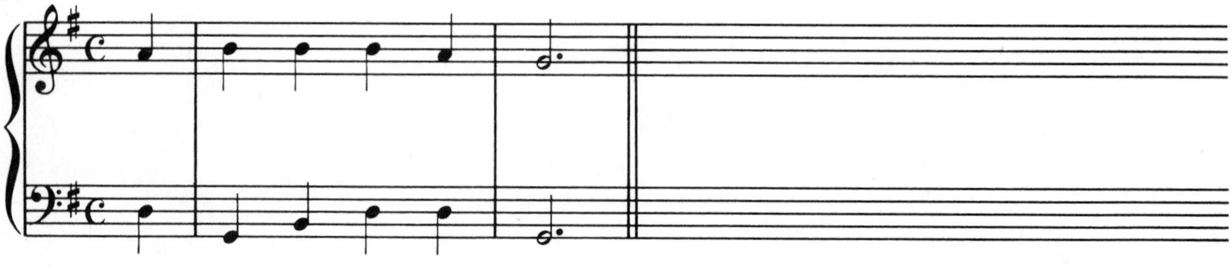

F. Analyze the chords specified by this figured bass. Then make two harmonizations, one for SAB chorus and one for SATB chorus.

1

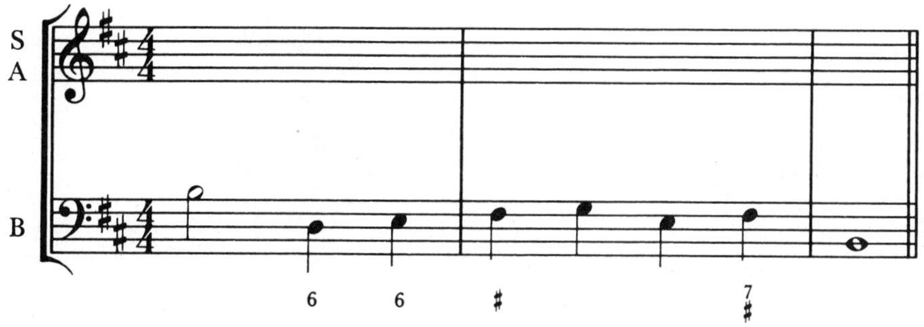

2

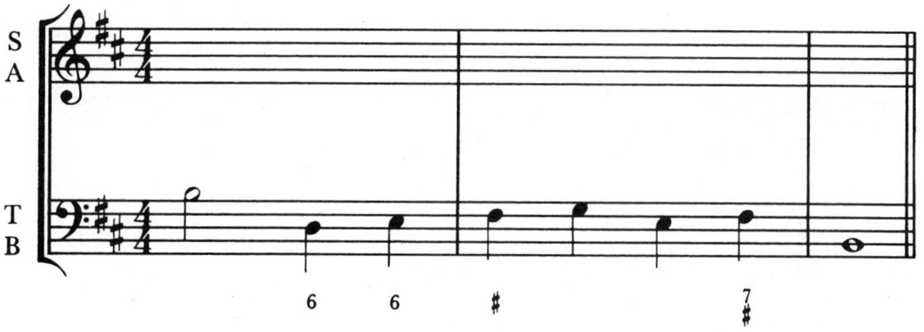

G. Analyze the chords implied by the soprano and bass lines below. Then fill in inner parts. Remember that the tenor part sounds a P8 lower than written.

H. Compose a period in a simple three-part texture. End the first phrase with a V^7-vi DC, the second with a V^7-I PAC. Then create a version for three instruments, the top part being elaborated by arpeggiations and NCTs, the other two parts in an accompanying role. Turn in both versions.

1. simple version

2. elaborated version

I. Set a short text for four-part chorus. The text might be a poem, a headline from a newspaper, anything. Include at least one V^7-I progression. Try to keep the motion going through the use of elaborations.

EXERCISE 12-2

A. Notate the specified chords. Use accidentals instead of key signatures.

1 2 3 4 5 6 7 8

D♭: V^{6}_{5} a: V^{4}_{3} E♭: V^{4}_{2} D: V^{4}_{3} c: V^{4}_{2} F: V^{6}_{5} b: V^{4}_{3} E: V^{6}_{5}

B. Label chords and NCTs in the excerpts below. Comment upon the treatment of the leading tone and 7th in any V^7 chords in root position or inversion.

1. Bach, "Ich dank' dir, lieber Herre"

(Which is the more sensible analysis of beat 4 of m. 3: iii^{6}_{4} or V^6?)

F:

2. Beethoven, Sonata Op. 2, No. 1, III

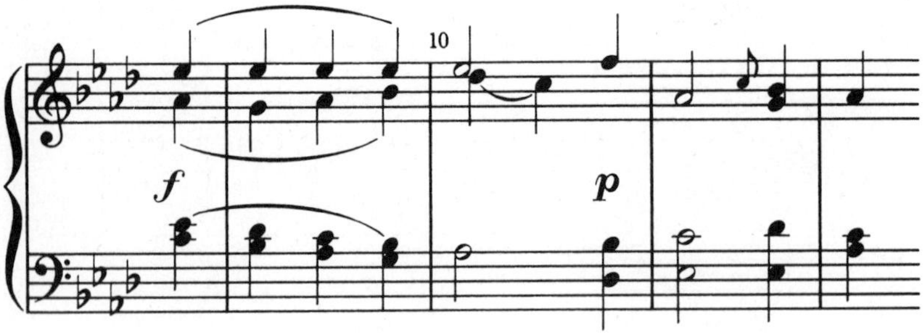

3. Mozart, Quintet K. 452, I (piano reduction)

B♭:

4. Schumann, "Im Westen," Op. 25, No. 23
(Do not label NCTs in this excerpt.)

C. Resolve each chord to a tonic triad (except as indicated). Analyze both chords.

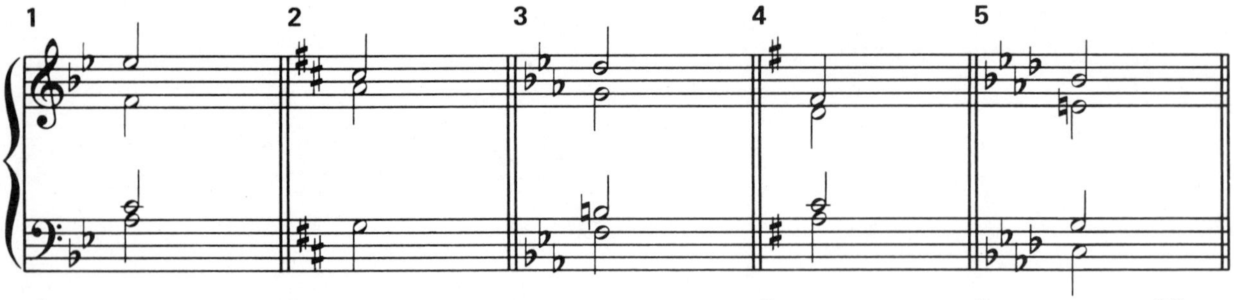

B♭: D: c: G: f: VI

C: f♯: f♯: g: A♭:

E♭: vi d: E: D♭: b:

D. Supply the key signature. Then notate and resolve the specified chord. Finally, begin the passage with a chord that will allow good voice leading and provide the indicated approach to the 7th. Notate as quarter notes. Label all unlabeled chords.

1 n | **2** p | **3** s | **4** app

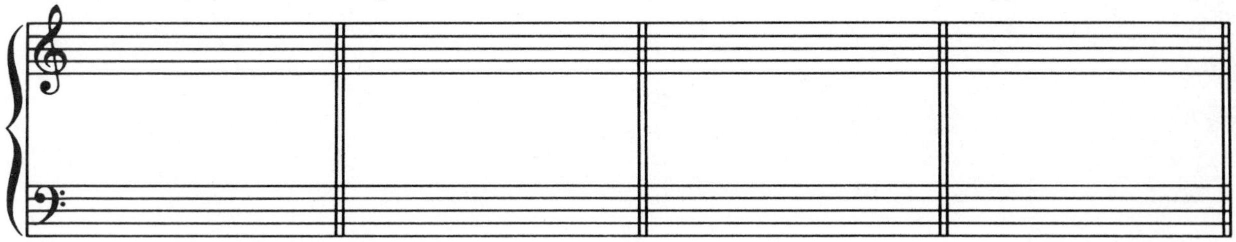

E♭: ___ V^6_5 ___ | g: ___ V^4_2 ___ | D: ___ V^7 ___ | b: ___ V^4_3 ___

5 s | **6** n | **7** s | **8** p

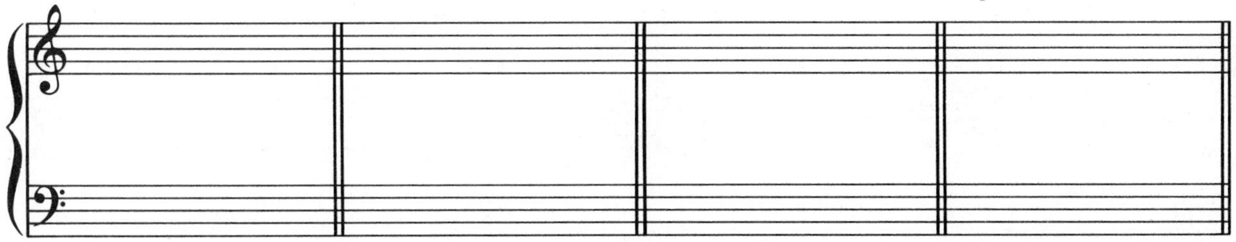

G: ___ V^7 vi | f: ___ V^6_5 ___ | B♭: ___ V^7 ___ | c♯: ___ V^4_3 i^6

9 app | **10** s | **11** p | **12** n

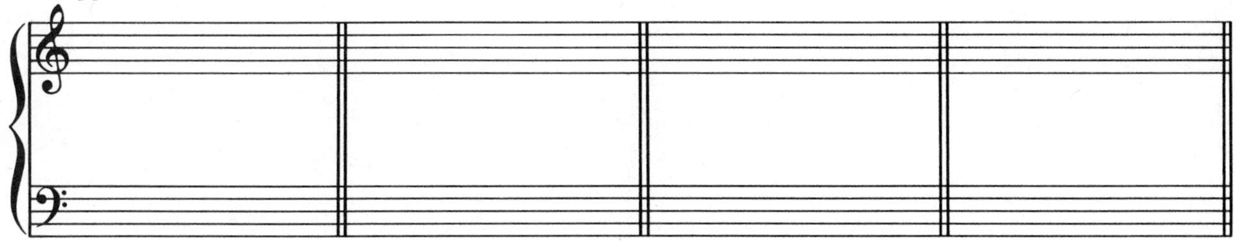

E: ___ V^7 ___ | c: ___ V^4_2 ___ | A♭: ___ V^4_3 I | f♯: ___ V^7 VI

E. Analyze the chords implied by each soprano/bass framework. Then add inner parts and embellishments to make a four-part choral texture. Include an inverted V^7 chord.

1

2

F. Analyze the chords implied by this soprano/bass framework. Then create a piano texture by filling out some of the chords and adding embellishments. Arpeggiations will be especially useful for prolonging the I chord in mm. 1-2. Be sure to include an inverted V^7 chord.

G. Make one or more settings of the following song.

1. Write an arrangement for two B♭ trumpets, unaccompanied. Analyze the harmonies implied by the two lines. Include at least one inverted V^7.
2. Make an arrangement for four-part chorus. Try to elaborate the other voices slightly. Include at least one inverted V^7. Watch out for parallel 8ves and 5ths throughout.
3. Compose a version for piano solo, including at least one inverted V^7. Be prepared to play it, or find someone else in the class who will do so.

H. Compose a period for a string trio (violin, viola, cello) or for some other combination of instruments in your class. Include at least two inverted V^7 chords.

CHAPTER THIRTEEN

THE II^{7} AND VII^{7} CHORDS

EXERCISE 13-1

A. Notate the following chords. Use accidentals, not key signatures.

1 2 3 4 5 6 7 8

g: vii$^{\circ 7}$ C: ii^{7} e: vii$^{\circ 4}_{2}$ E♭: ii$^{4}_{3}$ D: vii$^{\varnothing 6}_{5}$ f♯: ii$^{\varnothing 4}_{3}$ G: vii$^{\varnothing 7}$ A♭: ii^{7}

9 10 11 12 13 14 15 16

c: vii$^{\circ 6}_{5}$ d: ii$^{\varnothing 4}_{2}$ B♭: vii$^{\varnothing 6}_{5}$ b: ii$^{\varnothing 6}_{5}$ a: vii$^{\circ 6}_{5}$ A: ii$^{6}_{5}$ F: ii$^{4}_{2}$ c♯: vii$^{\circ 7}$

B. Analyze the following chords. Be sure your symbols indicate chord quality and inversion.

1 2 3 4 5 6 7 8

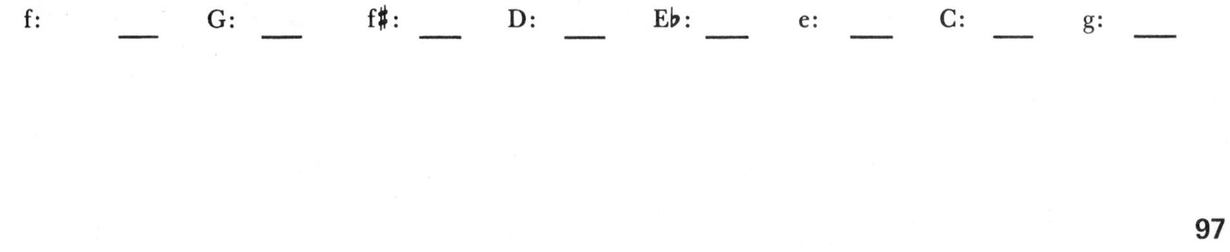

f: ___ G: ___ f♯: ___ D: ___ E♭: ___ e: ___ C: ___ g: ___

C. Analyze the chords and NCTs in the following excerpts. Whenever a ii^7 ($ii^{\varnothing 7}$) or $vii^{\varnothing 7}$ (vii^{o7}) chord is encountered, discuss the voice leading into and out of the chord.

1. Bach, "Jesu, der du meine Seele"

2. Bach, "Herzliebster Jesu, was hast du verbrochen"

b:

3. Mozart, Sonata K. 333, III

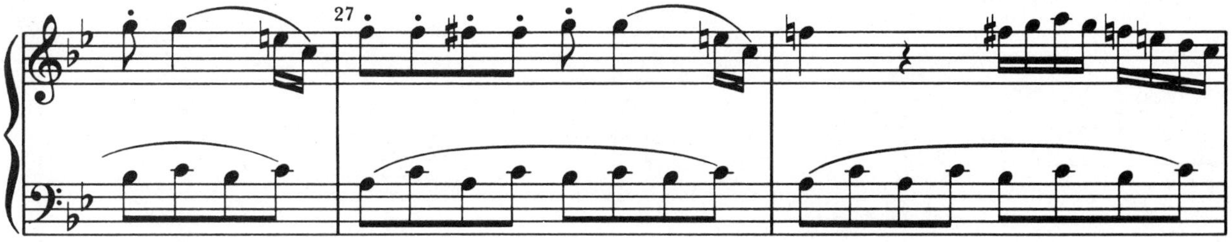

F:

4. Haydn, Quartet Op. 33, No. 3, III

C:

D. Notate, introduce, and resolve the specified chords. Approach each chord 7th as a suspension, a neighbor, or a passing tone, as specified. Include key signatures and roman numerals.

1 n **2** p **3** s **4** s

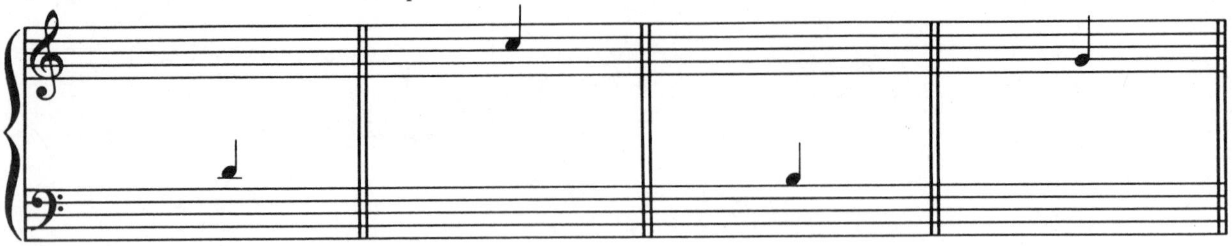

f♯: ___ vii$^{\circ 4}_{3}$ ___ C: ___ ii$^{6}_{5}$ ___ D: ___ vii$^{\varnothing 4}_{3}$ ___ g: ___ ii$^{\varnothing 7}$ ___

5 n **6** s **7** n **8** p

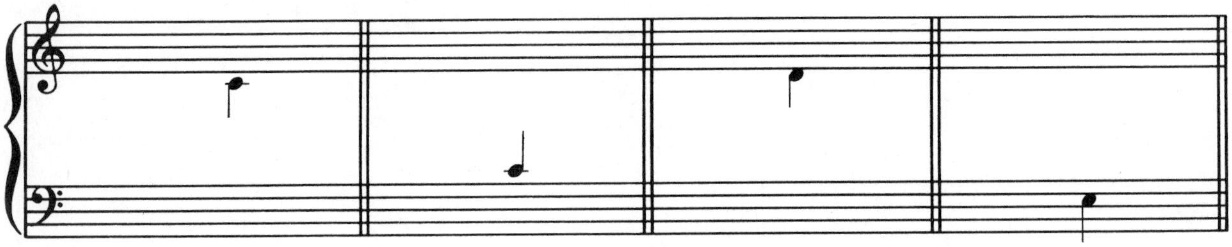

e: ___ vii$^{\circ 6}_{5}$ ___ c♯: ___ ii$^{\varnothing 4}_{3}$ ___ F: ___ vii$^{\varnothing 7}$ ___ E♭: ___ ii$^{4}_{2}$ ___

9 s **10** s **11** p **12** s

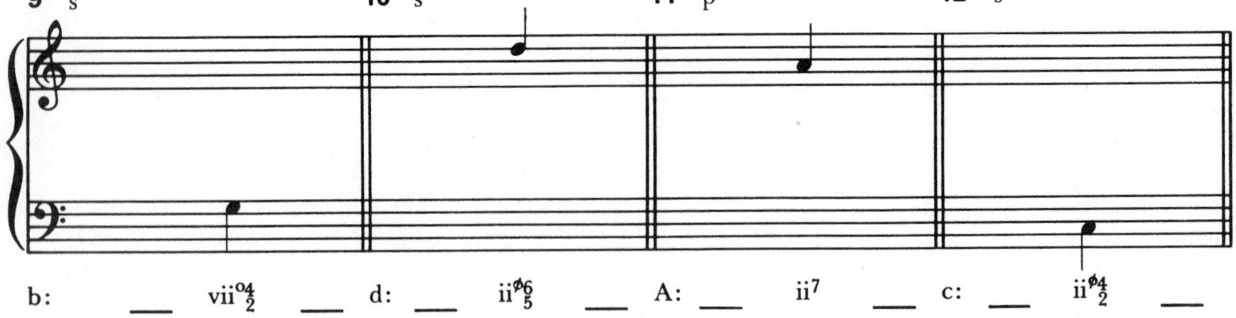

b: ___ vii$^{\circ 4}_{2}$ ___ d: ___ ii$^{\varnothing 6}_{5}$ ___ A: ___ ii^{7} ___ c: ___ ii$^{\varnothing 4}_{2}$ ___

E. Harmonize these chorale phrases for four-part chorus.

1. Include a root position ii^7.

G:

2. Include a root position vii^{o7} and a 4-3 suspension.

g:

3. Include a $ii^{ø4}_{2}$ and a deceptive cadence. Some eighth-note chords will be necessary.

d:

4. Include a $vii^{ø4}_{3}$ and a passing tone.

C:

F. Make a setting of the folk song below for some combination of voices and/or instruments available in your class. Include one of the chords discussed in this chapter.

CHAPTER FOURTEEN

OTHER DIATONIC SEVENTH CHORDS

EXERCISE 14-1

A. Notate the following chords. Use accidentals, not key signatures.

1 2 3 4 5 6 7 8

1	2	3	4	5	6	7	8
A♭: I^{M7}	g: $♯vi^{ø7}$	G: vi^{6}_{5}	f: III^{M6}_{5}	b: i^{7}	B♭: IV^{M4}_{3}	a: VI^{M7}	e: iv^{4}_{2}

9 10 11 12 13 14 15 16

9	10	11	12	13	14	15	16
E♭: IV^{M4}_{2}	c: i^{4}_{3}	c♯: IV^{7}	F: vi^{7}	E: I^{M6}_{5}	f♯: iv^{4}_{3}	d: VI^{M6}_{5}	A: iii^{4}_{2}

B. Analyze the following chords. Be sure your symbols indicate chord quality and inversion.

1 2 3 4 5 6 7 8

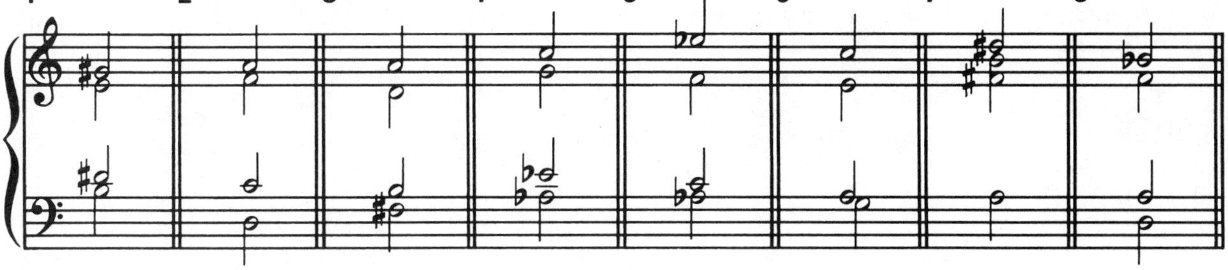

E: ___ a: ___ G: ___ E♭: ___ f: ___ C: ___ f♯: ___ d: ___

C. Analyze the chords in the excerpts below. Comment upon the voice leading involving any of the chords discussed in this chapter.

1. Schubert, *Moment Musical,* Op. 94, No. 6

Ab:

___ ___ ___ ___ ___
1 2 3 4 5

2. Bach, "Herr Jesu Christ, du höchstes Gut"

3. Haydn, Piano Sonata No. 30, I

After you finish labeling the chords, complete the three-part reduction of mm. 86-92 that follows the excerpt.

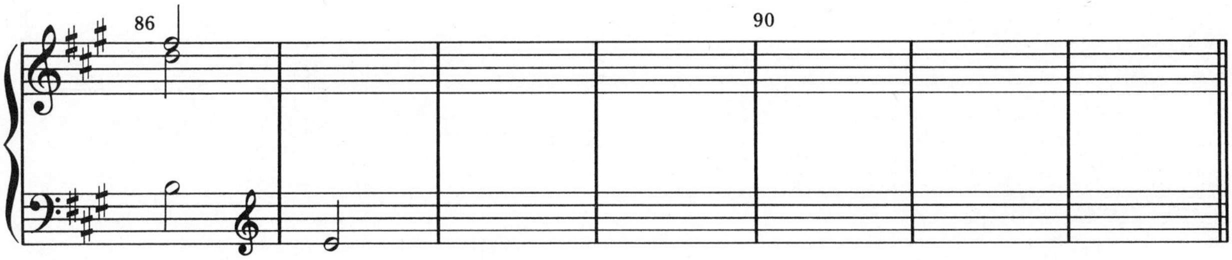

4. Corelli, Concerto Grosso Op. 6, No. 1, VII

D: iii

D. Continue this four-part elaboration of Example 14-19 (p. 232). Use B♮ throughout.

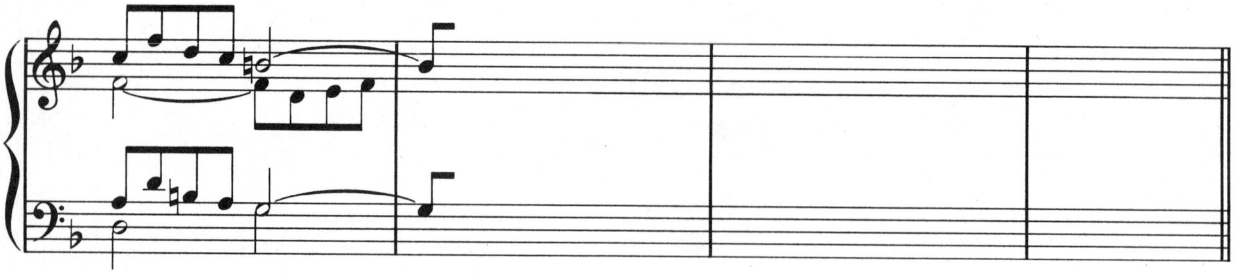

E. Notate, introduce, and resolve the specified chords. Approach each chord 7th as a suspension, a neighbor, or a passing tone, as specified. Include key signatures and roman numerals.

1 p **2** s **3** p **4** s

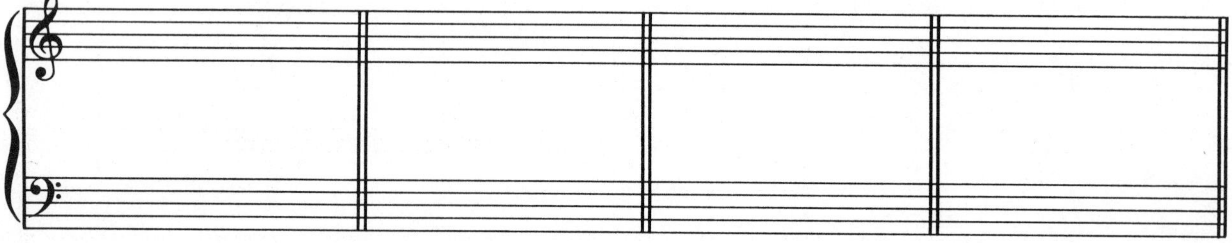

F: ___ iii^7 ___ E: ___ IV^{M6}_{5} ___ g: ___ i^6_5 ___ b: ___ $\sharp vi^{\phi 7}$ ___

5 n **6** s **7** p **8** s

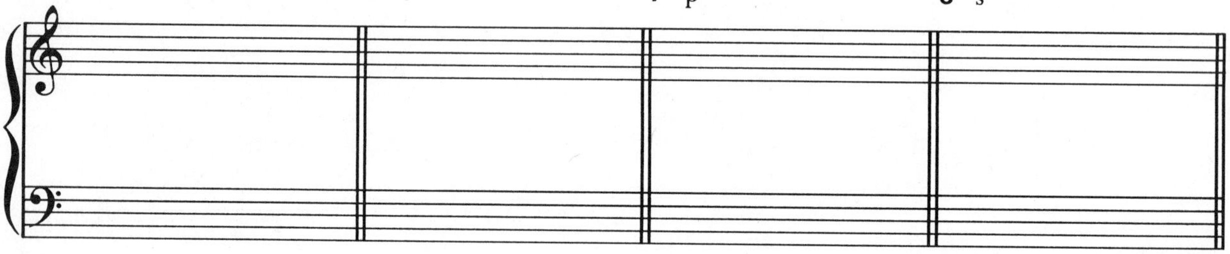

f: ___ III^{M7} ___ c♯: ___ iv^4_3 ___ E♭: ___ I^{M4}_{2} ___ D: ___ vi^7 ___

9 s **10** s **11** s **12** n

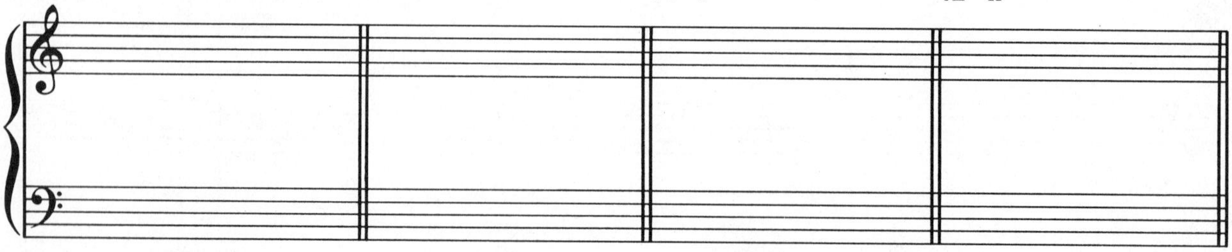

G: $\frac{6}{5}$ IV^{M4}_{2} $\frac{6}{5}$ c: $\overset{7}{\_\_\_}$ VI^{M4}_{3} $\overset{7}{\_\_\_}$ B♭: $\overset{7}{\_\_\_}$ I^{M7} $\overset{7}{\_\_\_}$ d: ___ IV^6_5 ___

(circle of fifths) (circle of fifths) (circle of fifths)

F. Analyze the chords called for by the figured bass below. Then continue the four-part realization of that figured bass. Note: be sure to review pages 231-232 before proceeding.

Corelli, Concerto Grosso Op. 6, No. 12, V

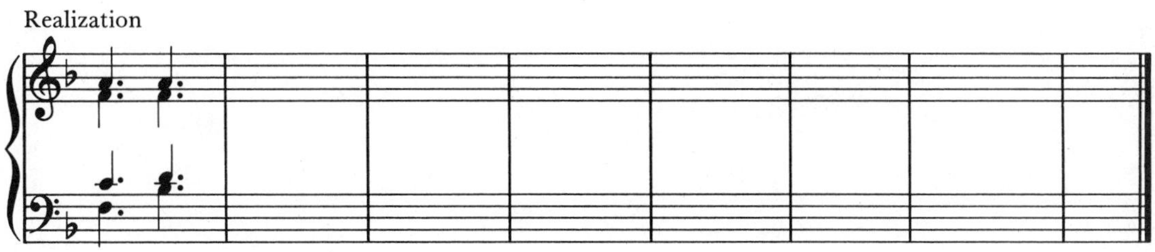

G. Compose a passage for three voices or instruments containing a sequence of seventh chords similar to that used in the excerpt of Part E.

H. The following is a simple note-against-note contrapuntal framework. Analyze the implied harmonies, then elaborate it into a passage containing several seventh chords. Use four parts or a free keyboard texture. Your final version might be complex, but the original framework should be retained. Include roman numerals and NCT analysis.

I. Create a framework similar to that above, but in the minor mode. Be sure that it implies a good harmonic progression. Then create an elaboration that employs some of the seventh chords discussed in this chapter. If possible, score for a combination of instruments in your class.

CHAPTER FIFTEEN

LEVELS OF HARMONY

EXERCISE 15-1

A. Analysis.

1. Label the chords and NCTs and do a levels analysis.

Bach, "Freu' dich sehr, o meine Seele"

2. This famous chorale was harmonized several times by Bach. Label the chords and NCTs and do a levels analysis. Analyze two chords on beat 3 of the first measure.

Bach, "O Haupt voll Blut und Wunden"

3. Label the chords and do a levels analysis. If you considered the F♯4 and the A3 at the end of the first measure to be chord tones, what would your analysis of that chord be? Does it make a sensible progression?

Bach, "Was Gott tut, das ist wohlgetan"

4. Label the chords and do a levels analysis. What is the form of this theme? Bracket two melodic sequences. Does the left hand take part in these sequences, or are they only melodic?

Beethoven, Rondo Op. 51, No. 1

B. Compose a phrase for piano with the following harmonic structure:

I	–	–	–	–	–	–	–	–	–	–	–	–	–	V
I	–	–	–	–	–	–	–	–	–	ii^6	–	–	–	V
I	–	–	–	–	–	–	–	I^6	–	ii^6	–	–	–	V
I	–	V^6_5	–	I	–	–	–	I^6	–	ii^6	–	–	–	V
I	–	V^6_5	–	I	–	IV^6	–	I^6	–	ii^6	–	I^6_4	–	V
													V	

C. Make up your own levels diagram similar to the one above, and compose a passage that expresses that harmonic structure.

CHAPTER SIXTEEN

SECONDARY FUNCTIONS 1

EXERCISE 16-1

A. Review the material on spelling secondary dominants (pp. 252-253). Then notate these secondary dominants in the specified inversions. Include key signatures.

1 | 2 | 3 | 4 | 5

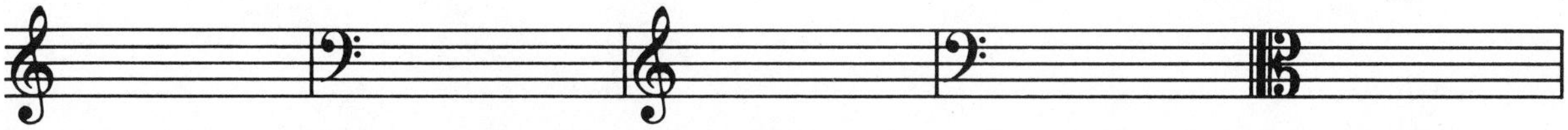

c♯: V^7/iv | A♭: V^6/V | c: V^4_3/VI | e: V^6/III | F: V^4_2/ii

6 | 7 | 8 | 9 | 10

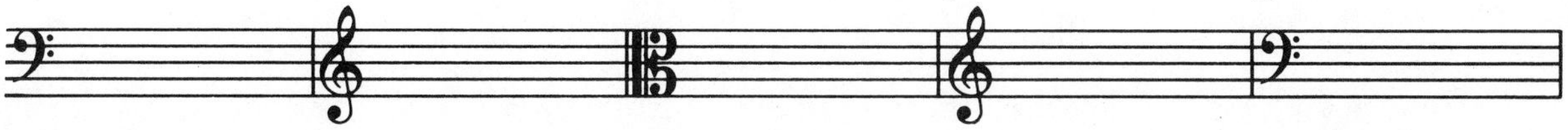

D: V^6/vi | b: V^7/V | A: V^6_5/iii | g: V/iv | a: V^4_2/V

11 | 12 | 13 | 14 | 15

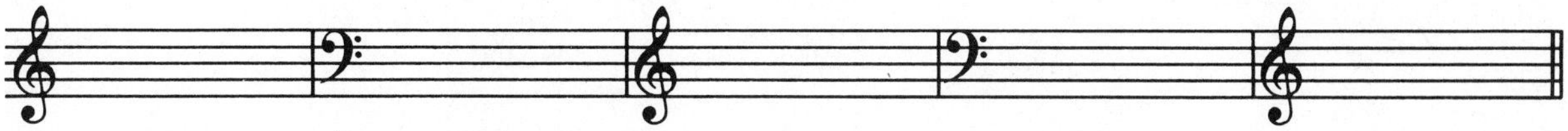

E♭: V^6_5/IV | f♯: V^6/VII | C: V^7/ii | B♭: V^4_2/IV | G: V^4_3/V

B. Label any chord that might be a secondary dominant according to the steps outlined on page 253. Label all others with an *x*.

f: ________ E: ________ C: ________ e: ________ g: ________

E♭: ________ f♯: ________ D: ________ F: ________ c: ________

A: ________ b: ________ d: ________ B♭: ________ G: ________

EXERCISE 16-2

A. Analysis.

1. Label chords and NCTs. Identify any six-four chords by type. This excerpt contains a set of parallel 5ths in a context that Bach must have found acceptable, since he used them so often in this situation. See if you can find them.

Bach, "Freuet euch, ihr Christen alle"

f:

2. Label chords and NCTs. Discuss the sequence implied by mm. 5-8. Is the excerpt an example of a period? If so, is it a parallel period or a contrasting period?

Beethoven, Sonata Op. 13, II

3. Label the chords with roman numerals. Thinking in terms of chord roots, find the longest harmonic sequence in this excerpt.

Beethoven, Sonata Op. 2, No. 1, I

4. Label chords and NCTs. Ignore the grace notes in your harmonic and NCT analysis; for example, the E♭5 in m. 1 is an upper neighbor ornamented by the appoggiatura grace note. Comment upon Chopin's use of F♯ and F♮ in this excerpt. Where do they occur? Are they ever in conflict? The form of the excerpt is a (parallel/contrasting) (period/double period).

Chopin, Mazurka Op. 67, No. 2

5. Label the chords with roman numerals. Label NCTs in the solo bassoon part only. The note under the fermata in m. 49 represents a V chord. It was at this point that the soloist improvised a cadenza. The conductor waited until he heard the soloist arrive at the G3 (often trilled), at which point he would signal the orchestra to be ready for their entrance in m. 50.

Mozart, Bassoon Concerto K. 191, II

45
Ob.
Hn. in F
Bsn.
Vl. I
Vl. II
Vla.
Vc. D.B.

49
50
Ob.
Hn. in F
Bsn.
Vl. I
Vl. II
Vla.
Vc. D.B.

6. Label chords and NCTs. What is the form of this excerpt? (Note: mm. 1-2 are introductory.)

Beethoven, Quartet Op. 135, III

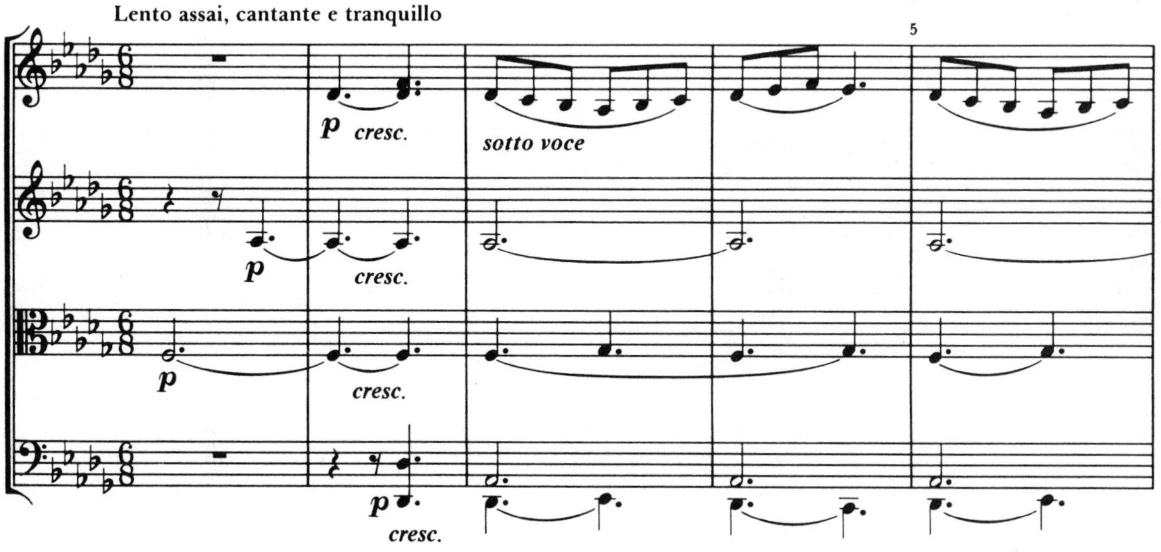

B. For each of the following problems, first analyze the given chord. Next, find a smooth way to lead into the chord. While there are many possibilities, it will often work to use a chord whose root is a P5 above the root of the secondary dominant. Experiment with other relationships also. Then resolve each chord properly, taking special care with the leading tone and 7th resolutions. Analyze all chords.

g: ___ ___ ___ C: ___ ___ ___ G: ___ ___ V^6_5/V E: ___ ___ ___ A♭: ___ ___ ___

D: ___ ___ ___ B♭: ___ ___ ii^7 f: ___ ___ ___ c: ___ ___ ___ a: ___ ___ ___

C. List below each note the secondary V and V⁷ chords that could harmonize that note. You may find it helpful to refer to the charts on page 251.

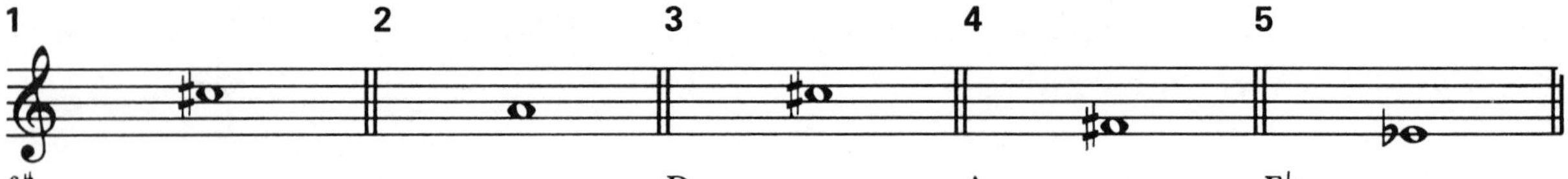

f♯: e: D: A: E♭:

b: B♭: d: F: A♭:

D. Provide roman numerals to show how the first note could be harmonized as a secondary dominant. The second note should be harmonized by the tonicized chord.

E. Analyze the chords specified by each figured bass, then make an arrangement for SATB chorus. Strive for smooth voice leading, even if this results in a dull soprano line.

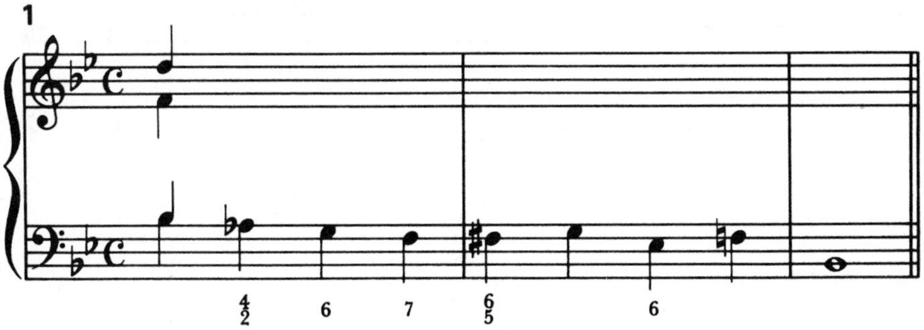

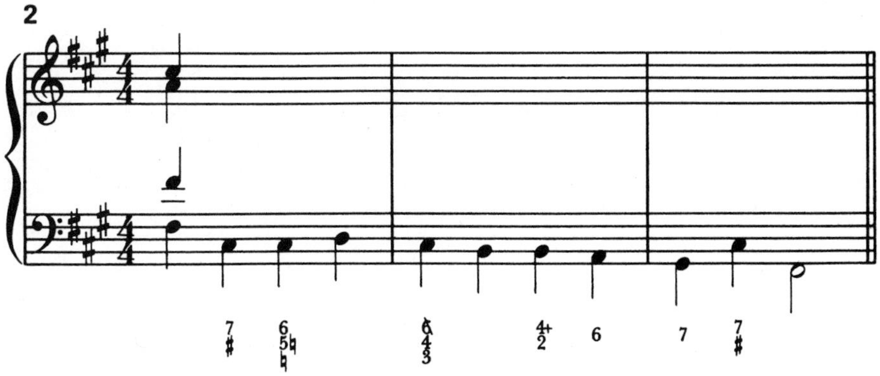

F. Harmonize each chorale phrase for SATB chorus. Include one or more secondary dominants in each phrase, and activate the texture with some NCTs.

1

E♭:

2

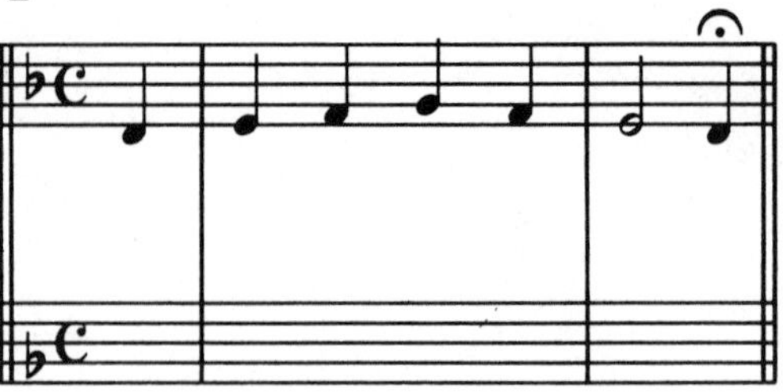

d:

3

C:

4

g:

G. Analyze the harmonies implied by the following soprano/bass framework. Then make a more interesting version for piano, beginning with the two measures given below.

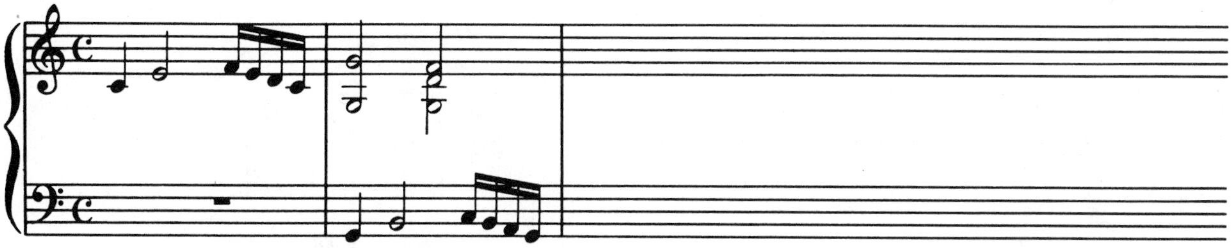

H. Continue the example below to make a total of at least eight measures. Include one or more secondary dominants, and end with a PAC. Then score it for four instruments found in your class. Analyze all chords and NCTs.

I. Finish the analysis of the phrase below. This phrase is to serve as the *a* phrase of a longer theme you will compose. The theme will be in the form of a parallel double period. Include at least one secondary dominant.

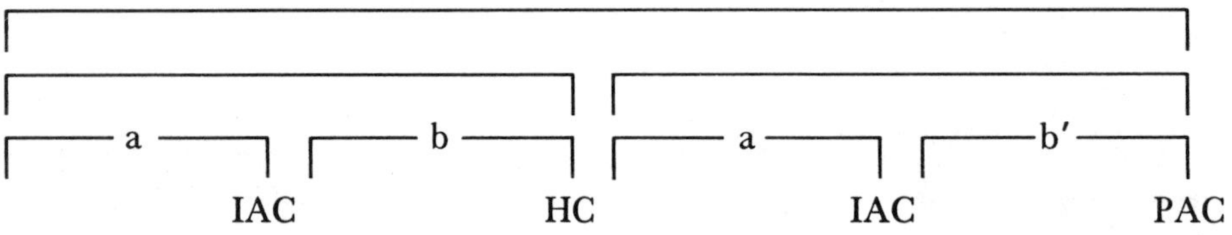

CHAPTER SEVENTEEN

SECONDARY FUNCTIONS 2

EXERCISE 17-1

A. Review how to spell secondary leading-tone chords (p. 268). Then notate these secondary leading-tone chords in the specified inversion. Include key signatures.

1 2 3 4 5

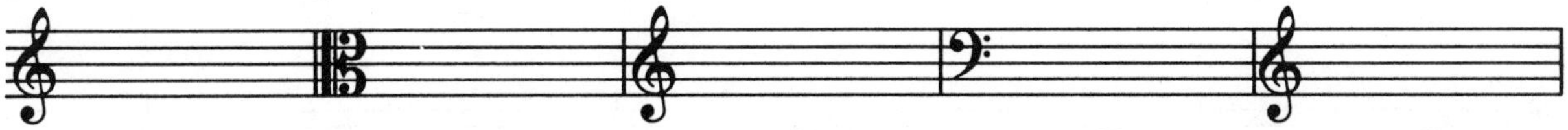

A: vii^{o6}/iii F: vii^{o6}/ii c: vii^{o6}/VI E: vii$^{o6}_{5}$/IV A♭: vii^{o7}/IV

6 7 8 9 10

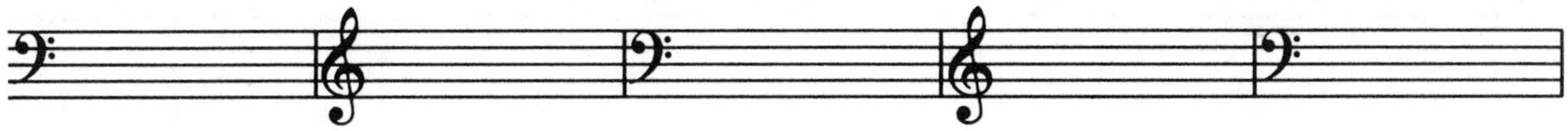

d: vii$^{o6}_{5}$/V G: vii^{o7}/vi B♭: vii^{o6}/vi g: vii^{o7}/VII F: vii^{o7}/ii

11 12 13 14 15

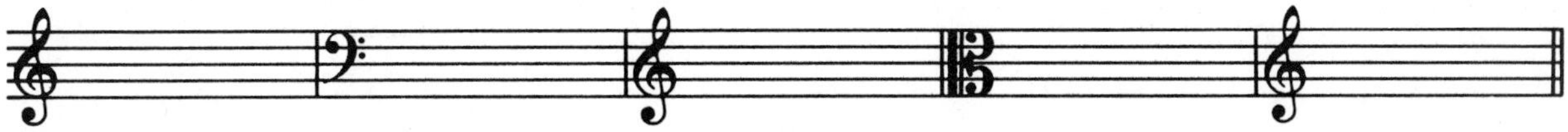

C: vii$^{ø4}_{2}$/V e: vii^{o6}/iv E♭: vii$^{ø4}_{3}$/V f♯: vii^{o7}/III D: vii^{o6}/V

B. Label any chord that would be a secondary leading-tone chord according to the steps outlined on page 268. Label all others with an *x*.

1 2 3 4 5

c: ________ G: ________ A: ________ B♭: ________ e: ________

6 7 8 9 10

C: ________ d: ________ E: ________ E♭: ________ A♭: ________

11 12 13 14 15

F: ________ f♯: ________ D: ________ C: ________ c♯: ________

EXERCISE 17-2

A. Analysis.

1. Label the chords with roman numerals. How much of this excerpt is devoted to circle-of-fifths progressions?

Schubert, "Wohin?," Op. 25, No. 2

2. Analyze chords and NCTs.

Bach, *Well-Tempered Clavier,* Book II, Prelude 12

3. Label the chords with roman numerals (the Italian augmented sixth chord in m. 4 will be discussed in Chapter 23). Use your imagination, and your ear, in analyzing the last chord in m. 2.

Schumann, "Die Löwenbraut," Op. 31, No. 1

4. Label chords and NCTs. (An optional piano accompaniment is omitted from the example.) What is the form of this excerpt?

Brahms, "Und gehst du über den Kirchhof"

5. Analyze chords and NCTs. Find two circle-of-fifths progressions that contain more than four chords. What is the form of this excerpt?

Tchaikovsky, "Morning Prayer," Op. 39, No. 1

6. This short song is given here in its entirety. Analyze the chords and NCTs. There are some places where alternative analyses are possible—in m. 1, for example, where the line G♯-F♯-E could be analyzed as chord tones or as passing tones. Think of two analyses for the second chord in m. 11, one of them being a secondary function.

Schumann, "Aus meinen Thranen Spriessen," Op. 48, No. 2

B. For each of these problems, first analyze and resolve the given chord, being especially careful with the chord 7th and the leading tone. Then find a smooth way to lead into the given chord. Analyze all chords.

1 2 3 4 5

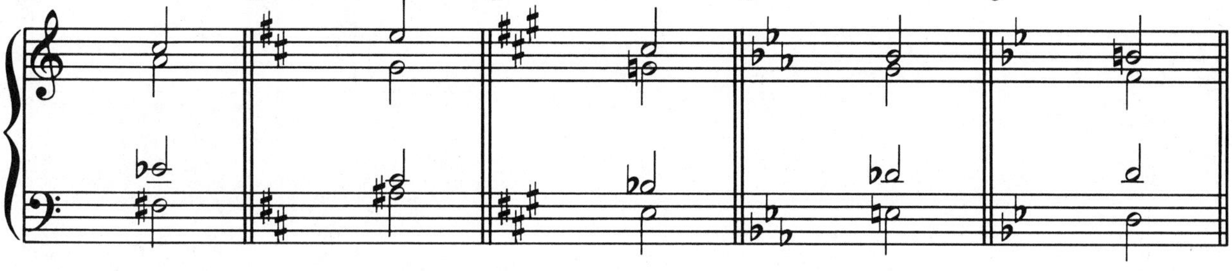

C: ___ ___ ___ D: ___ ___ ___ A: ___ ___ ___ E♭: ___ ___ ___ B♭: ___ ___ ___

6 7 8 9 10

E: ___ ___ ___ c: ___ ___ ___ f: ___ ___ ___ g: ___ ___ ___ F: ___ ___ ___

C. Analyze the harmonies specified by each figured bass, and make an arrangement for SATB chorus. Try to use smooth voice leading, even at the expense of an interesting soprano line.

1

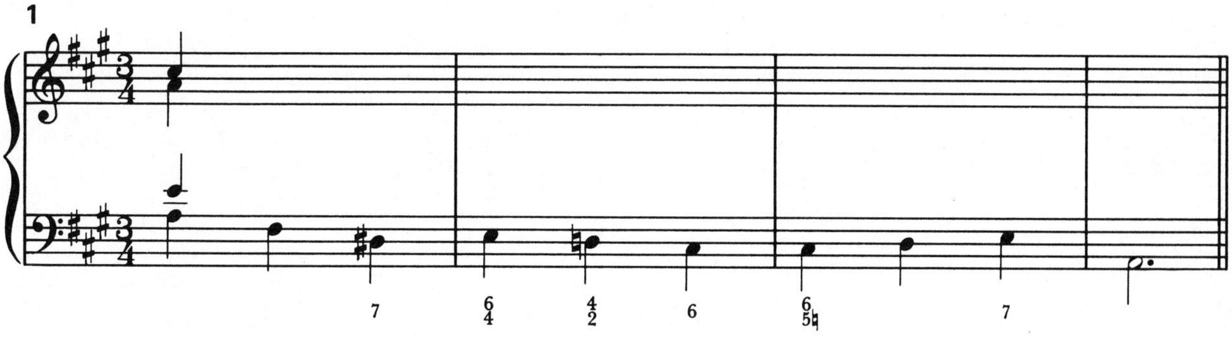

2

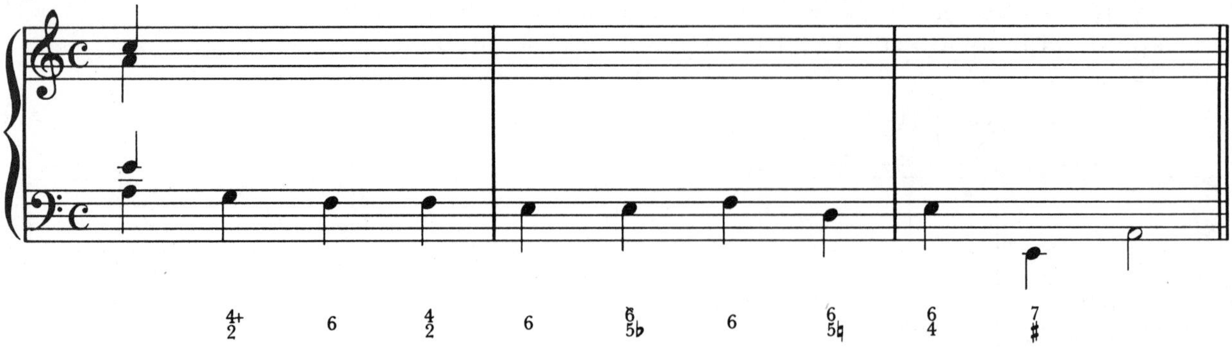

D. Harmonize each of these chorale phrases for SATB chorus. Include at least one secondary leading-tone chord or incorporate some other aspect discussed in this chapter in each harmonization.

1 2

F: a:

3

F:

E. Each item below contains two versions of the same excerpt, one of them in a simple texture and one more elaborate. Continue the simple texture first, including some aspect of harmony discussed in this chapter. Then continue the elaboration, using your simple version as a framework. Label chords and NCTs.

1a.

1b.

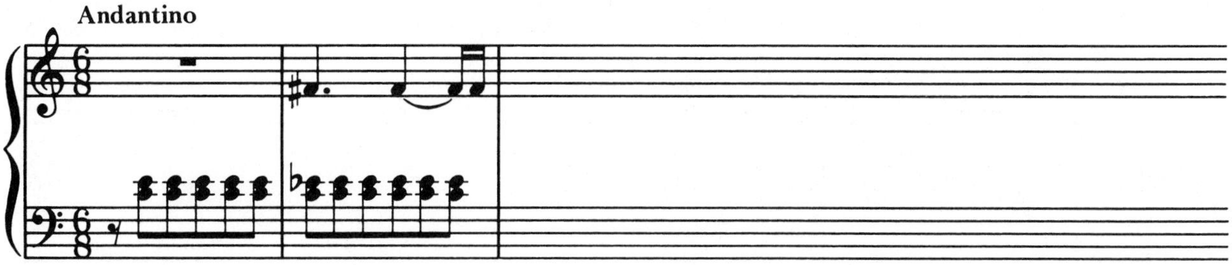

2a.

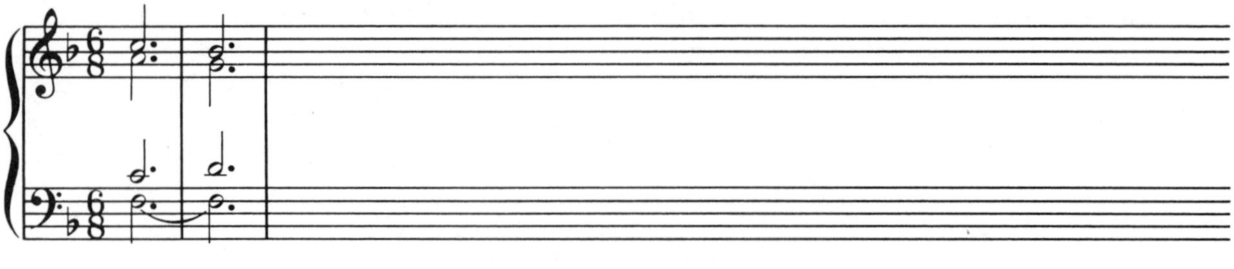

2b.

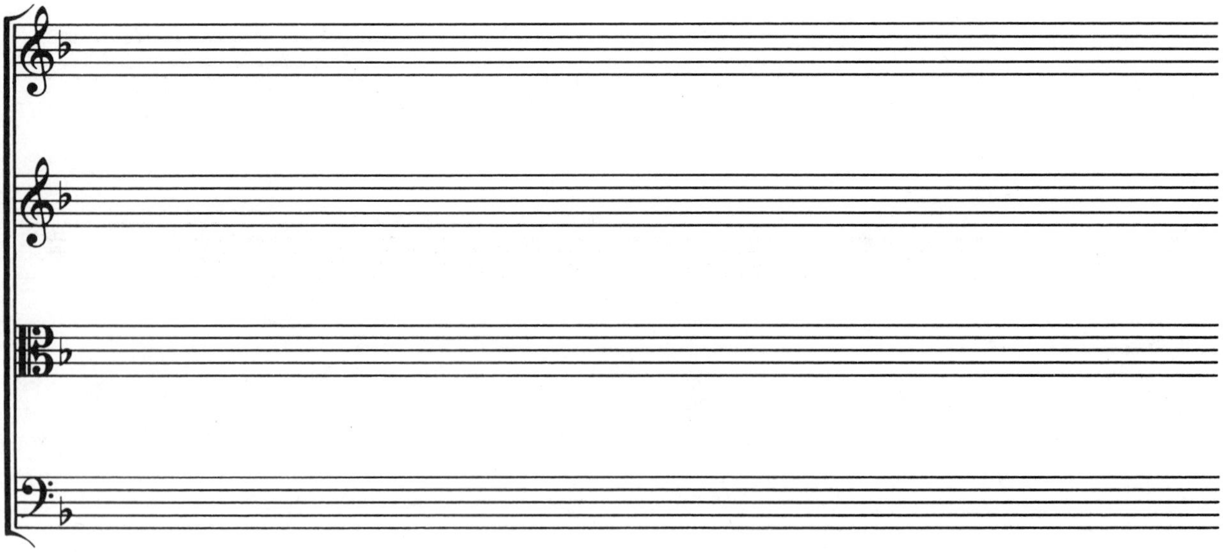

F. Compose a setting of the following poem for chorus (three, four, or five parts) or for solo voice with piano accompaniment. Use at least one secondary leading-tone chord and one deceptive resolution of a secondary dominant. Try to put your special harmonic effects at appropriate places in the text. (Use either or both stanzas.)

A bird came down the walk;
He did not know I saw;
He bit an angle-worm in halves
And ate the fellow raw.

And then he drank a dew
From a convenient grass,
And then hopped sidewise to the wall
To let a beetle pass.

CHAPTER EIGHTEEN

MODULATIONS USING DIATONIC COMMON CHORDS

EXERCISE 18-1

A. Name the relative key in each case.

1. G♭ ____
2. A ____
3. e ____
4. g ____
5. C♯ ____
6. d ____
7. F♯ ____
8. c♯ ____
9. A♭ ____
10. a♭ ____

B. Name all the keys closely related to the given key. Be sure to use upper case for major, lower case for minor.

1. b ____ ____ ____ ____ ____
2. e♭ ____ ____ ____ ____ ____
3. G ____ ____ ____ ____ ____
4. B ____ ____ ____ ____ ____
5. F ____ ____ ____ ____ ____
6. f♯ ____ ____ ____ ____ ____

C. Name the relationship in each case (enharmonically equivalent; parallel; relative and closely related; closely related; foreign).

1. D/e ________________
2. e♭/G♭ ________________
3. A/a ________________
4. d♯/G ________________
5. B♭/F ________________
6. A♭/C♭ ________________
7. C♯/D♭ ________________
8. g♯/c♯ ________________
9. a♭/b♭ ________________
10. c/E♭ ________________

EXERCISE 18-2

A. Analysis.

1. Label chords and NCTs in this chorale, which is presented in its entirety. Which two phrases are very similar melodically? What portion of these phrases is harmonized similarly? What chord is emphasized in the first half of the second of these two phrases?

Bach, "Uns ist ein Kindlein heut' geborn"

2. This example, also a complete chorale, is in g minor, although it ends with a major triad (the "Picardy third"). Label chords and NCTs. Notice how often the melody follows an arch contour (inverted in the second phrase). Bracket those arch contours in the melody. If you find any similar contours in the bass, bracket them also.

Bach, "Jesu, der du meine Seele"

3. Label the chords with roman numerals. How do the pickup notes at the beginning of the excerpt help smooth the return to the first key when the repeat is taken?

Mozart, Sonata K. 330, II

4. Listen to this song all the way through. Then list every tonality that is touched upon in the song, either by simple tonicization or by modulation. Which (other than tonic) is referred to again at the end of the song? Decide upon one or two tonalities (other than tonic) that represent modulations rather than tonicizations. Then label all chords with roman numerals.

Schumann, "Wenn ich in deine Augen seh'," Op. 48, No. 4

10
sund. Wenn ich mich lehn' an dei - ne Brust, kommt's ü - ber ruich wie Him - mels -
Ped.
ritard.
15
lust; doch wenn du sprichst: Ich lie - be dich, so muss ich wei - nen bit - ter -
ritard.
20
lich.
rit.
ritard.
p
pp

5. Label chords and NCTs in this excerpt. Then look back at the other song passages in the Exercise and Self-Test sections of this chapter. Does the piano double the vocal line in all cases? In which one is the vocal part most independent of the accompaniment? Try to rank them from most doubled to most independent.

Beethoven, "Resignation"

6. Label the chords with roman numerals. In an Alberti bass accompaniment, such as the left hand in this example, the bass note for each chord is usually considered to be the lowest note struck. So in m. 9 the only *bass* notes are D and C♯.

Beethoven, Sonata Op. 10, No. 3, II

B. Fill in the name of the new key on the second line of each exercise.

1. e: i $ii^{\circ 6}$ V^4_2 i^6 iv^6

___: i^6 V^4_2 i^6 $ii^{\circ 6}$ V^7 i

2. D: I V I^6 $vii^{\circ 6}$

___: $ii^{\circ 6}$ i^6_4 V i

V

3. F: I $vii^{\circ 6}$ I^6 vi

___: ii $vii^{\circ 6}$ I V^6_5 I

4. g: i V^6_5 V^4_2/iv iv^6 V i^6

___: iv^6 $ii^{\circ 6}$ V^7 i

5. b: i $ii^{\varnothing 4}_{\ 2}$ V^6_5 i VI iv^6

___: ii^6 I^6_4 V^7 I

V

6. E♭: I ii^6 V vi

___: iv $ii^{\varnothing 6}_{\ 5}$ V VI iv V i

7. A: I V^4_3 I^6 V^6

___: IV^6 V^6_5 i $ii^{\varnothing 6}_{\ 5}$ i^6_4 V^7 i

8. c: i V^7 VI iv

___: vi IV^6 I^6_4 ii^6_5 V I

C. List the diatonic triads that could serve as common chords between each pair of keys. In minor keys, assume the usual chord qualities: i, ii°, III, iv, V, VI, vii°.

ex. First key, C:	I	iii	V	vi
Triads:	C	e	G	a
Second key, G:	IV	vi	I	ii

1. First key, E:
Triads:
Second key, f♯:

2. First key, D♭:
Triads:
Second key, G♭:

3. First key, c:
Triads:
Second key, B♭:

4. First key, f:
Triads:
Second key, A♭:

5. First key, B:
Triads:
Second key, F♯:

6. First key, A♭:
Triads:
Second key, B♭:

D. Choose two of the progressions from Part B. Arrange one for SATB chorus and the other for SAB chorus. Activate the texture with NCTs and/or arpeggiations. Arrange the metric and rhythmic structure so that the last chord comes on a strong beat. Label chords and NCTs.

E. Harmonize the following chorale tunes for SATB chorus.

1. In the first phrase, modulate from i to III. The second phrase should return to i.

2. Modulate from I to vi in phrase 1. Return to I in phrase 2.

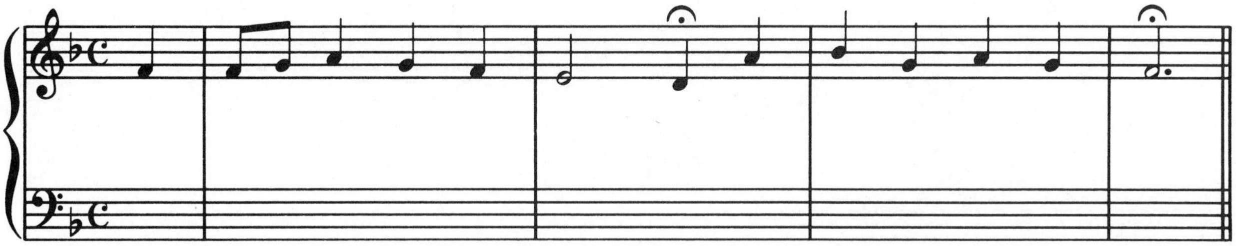

F. Analyze the chords specified by this figured bass, and then make an arrangement for SATB chorus.

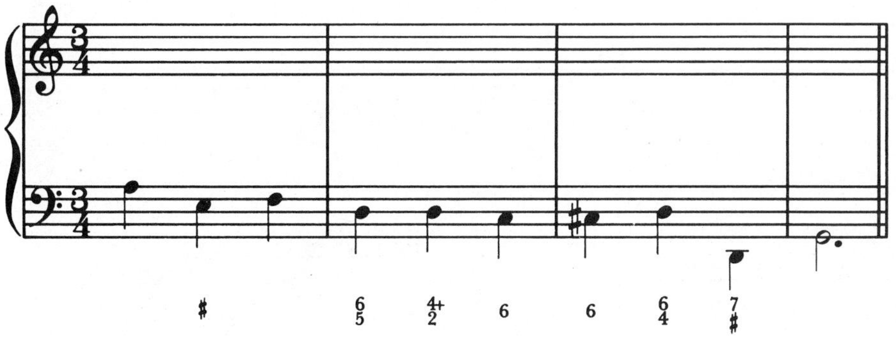

G. Continue this soprano/bass framework, analyzing the implied harmonies. Phrase 1 (mm. 1-4) should end with a HC in f. Phrase 2 (mm. 5-8) should end with a PAC in A♭. The resulting form is a modulating period. Then arrange for some combination of instruments in your class, filling in as many inner parts as needed. Elaborate your final version with NCTs and arpeggiations.

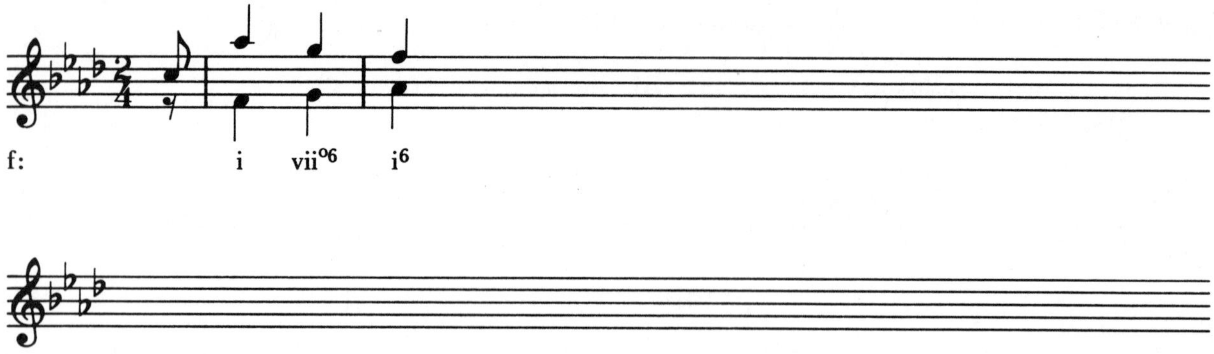
f:
i
vii°6
i6

H. Compose a double period for some solo instrument with piano accompaniment. As the diagram indicates, the first phrase stays in A, while the second tonicizes (or modulates to) E. Phrase 3 returns briefly to A but turns quickly to D. The fourth phrase returns to A for the final cadence.

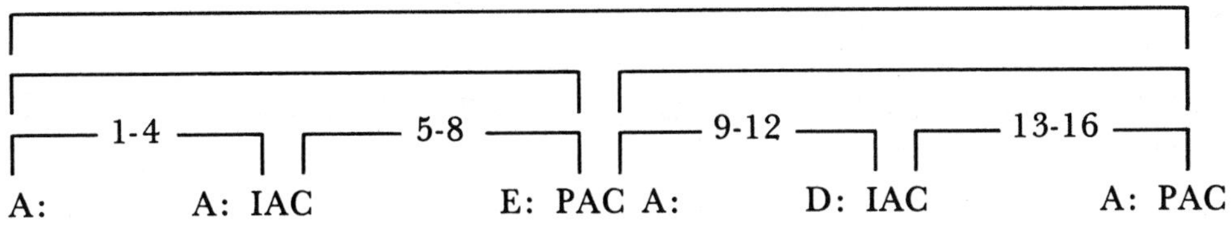

Or, in the larger view:

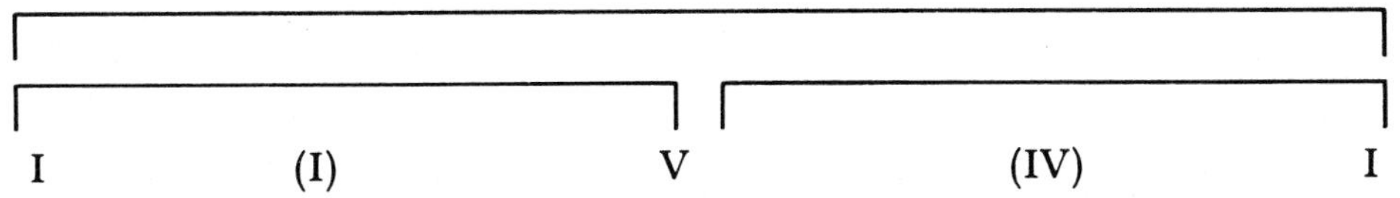

The beginning of phrase 1 is given below. Compose the soprano/bass framework first.

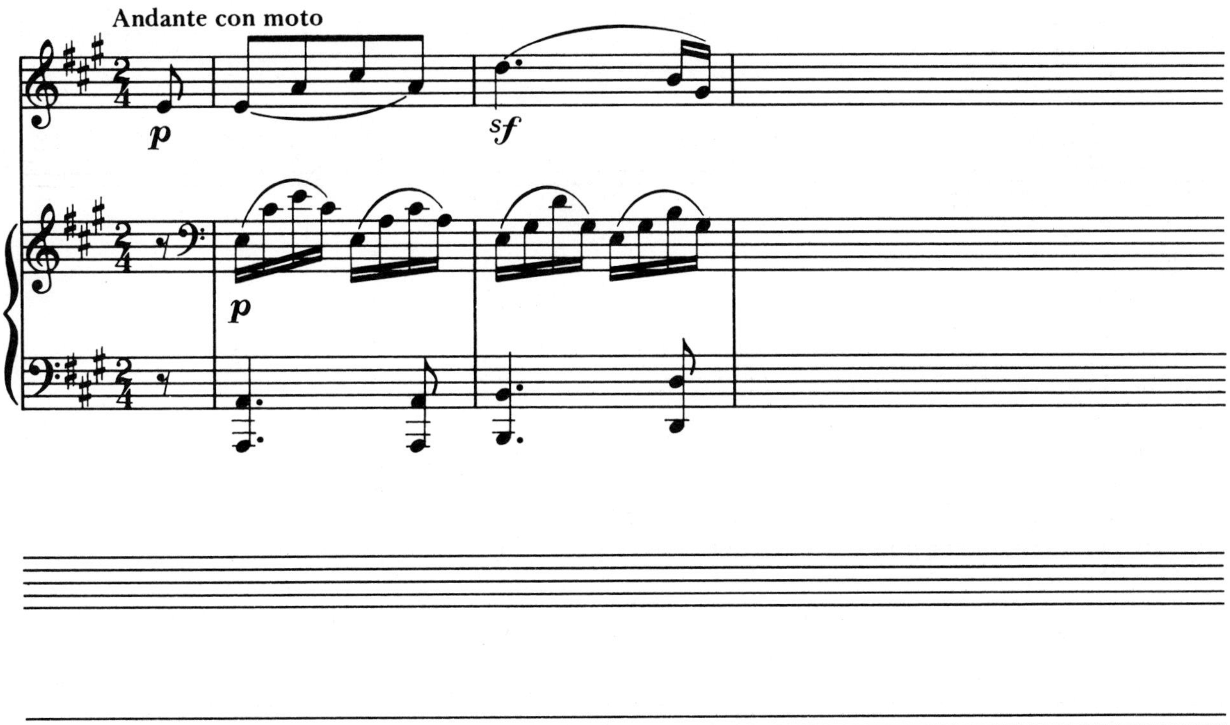

I. Using a text of your own choosing, compose a passage for chorus (three or four parts). If in major, it should have a tonal scheme of I-vi-I-ii-I. If in minor, use i-VI-i-iv-i.

CHAPTER NINETEEN

SOME OTHER MODULATORY TECHNIQUES

EXERCISE 19-1

A. Analysis. (Note: Some of the modulations below may be of the diatonic common-chord type.)

1. What two keys are implied in this excerpt? Describe how the change of key takes place?

Schubert, "Zur guten Nacht"

2. There are two modulations in this excerpt. Label chords and NCTs. At what point does Bach not follow the conventions of spacing discussed on page 74? What is achieved by the spacing he uses? Where is there a sonority used in an unusual bass position? How is the reason for this bass position related to the question about the spacing?

Bach, "Warum betrübst du dich"

3. What two keys are found in this excerpt? How are they related? What is the best way to describe the modulation?

Schubert, "Valse sentimentale," Op. 50, No. 13

4. Two distantly related keys are found in this passage. Label chords and NCTs.

Schubert, "Auf dem Flusse," Op. 89, No. 7

5. This excerpt touches upon three tonalities. Identify the tonalities and the modulatory means employed, and label the chords with roman numerals.

Beethoven, Symphony No. 1, Op. 21, I

B. Analyze the harmonies implied by this soprano/bass framework. Add an alto part to create a three-part texture. Embellish the texture with a few NCTs, including a 4-3 suspension. Identify the modulatory technique used.

C. Analyze the implied harmonies, and then add alto and tenor parts. Enliven the texture with NCTs and/or arpeggiations. Identify the modulatory technique used.

D. Use the framework below as the basis for a repeated period. The second phrase should begin and end in D major (phrase modulation). Compose a first ending that modulates back to F using some modulatory technique discussed in this chapter. Include NCTs and arpeggiations in your final version. Score for piano or some combination of instruments found in your class.

E. The framework below is also to be used as the basis for a repeated period for piano (or other instruments). The first phrase is in E♭ and the second should be a sequential repetition of the first, in A♭. Write out the repeat of phrases 1-2. Use more embellishments in the repeat than you used in the first eight measures.

CHAPTER TWENTY

BINARY AND TERNARY FORMS

EXERCISE 20-1

A. Diagram this excerpt down to the phrase level and name the form. Assume all phrases are four measures long. Also, answer the following questions:

1. Where is there a vii^{ø7} over a tonic pedal point?
2. What chord is the basis of mm. 9-12?
3. Label the chords in mm. 13-16.

Mozart, *Eine kleine Nachtmusik*, K. 525, II

B. Name the form of this piece (do not diagram phrases and cadences). Watch out for written-out repeats. Also, do or answer the following:

1. Label the chords in mm. 5-8.
2. What chord forms the basis of mm. 33-39?
3. Analyze the last chord in m. 34.
4. In what measures does the "boom-chick-chick" accompaniment drop out?

Chopin, Mazurka Op. 67, No. 3

a tempo
p
20
tr
Ped.
25
30
cresc.
sf
ff poco rit.
a tempo
ten.
sf
pp
35

ten.
40
a tempo
sf
riten.
p
tr
45
50
cresc.
sf
55
ff poco rit.
Ped.

C. Diagram this piece down to the phrase level and name the form. Also, answer the following questions:

1. Where is a sequence involving both hands? Bracket it.
2. What does the G♯4 in m. 6 accomplish?
3. What material in mm. 10-22 is obviously derived from mm. 1-9?

March from the *Notebook for Anna Magdalena Bach*

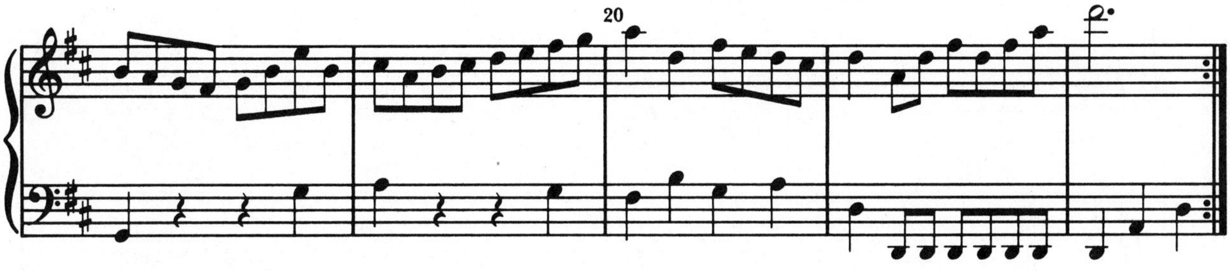

D. Diagram this choral excerpt down to the phrase level and name the form. (Note: mm. 229-44 are actually repeated, but this does not change your analysis.) Assume the phrases are eight measures long. Also, do the following:

1. Label these chords in the key of D:

m. 222, beat 2 ____ m. 234, beat 2 ____ m. 235, beat 2 ____

2. Find consecutive 5ths by contrary motion.

3. Find consecutive 8ves by contrary motion.

4. Find a 4-3 suspension.

Beethoven, Symphony No. 9, Op. 125, IV (chorus and low strings only)

225
230
sf
S.
Himm - li - sche, dein Hei - lig - tum! Dei - ne Zau - ber
A.
Himm - li - sche, dein Hei - lig - tum! Dei - ne Zau - ber
T.
Himm - li - sche, dein Hei - lig - tum! Dei - ne Zau - ber
B.
Himm - li - sche, dein Hei - lig - tum! Dei - ne Zau - ber
Vc.
D.B.

235
ff
S.
bin - den wie - der, was die Mo - de streng ge - teilt; al -
A.
bin - den wie - der, was die Mo - de streng ge - teilt; al -
T.
bin den wie der, was die Mo - de streng ge - teilt; al -
B.
bin - den wie - der, was die Mo - de streng ge - teilt; al -
Vc.
D.B.

240
S.
A.
T.
B.
Vc.
D.B.
sf
- le Men - schen wer - den Brü - der wo dein sanf - ter
- le Men - schen wer - den Brü - der wo dein sanf - ter
- le Men - schen_ wer - den Brü - der wo dein sanf - ter
- le Men - schen wer - den Brü - der wo dein sanf - ter

S.
A.
T.
B.
Vc.
D.B.
Flü - gel weilt.
Flü - gel weilt.
Flü - gel weilt.
Flü - gel weilt.

CHAPTER TWENTY-ONE

MODE MIXTURE

EXERCISE 21-1

A. Notate these chords in the specified inversions. Include key signatures.

1 2 3 4 5

A: $\text{ii}^{\varnothing 4}_{2}$ F: $\text{vii}^{\circ 7}$ D♭: i^{6}_{4} C: ♭VI E: $\text{ii}^{\circ 6}$

6 7 8 9 10

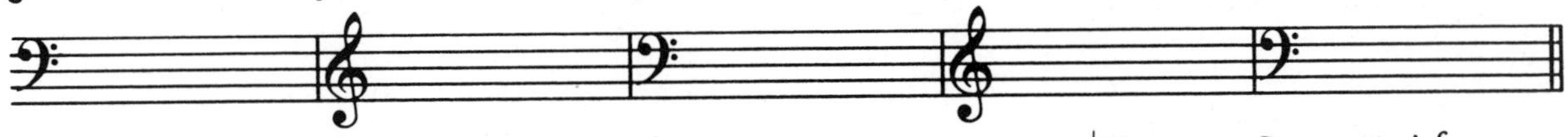

A♭: $\text{vii}^{\circ 6}_{5}$ E♭: iv f♯: I D: ♭III G: iv^{6}

B. Label these chords. Include inversion symbols.

1 2 3 4 5

F: ___ D: ___ B♭: ___ A: ___ A♭: ___

C. Analysis.

1. Label the chords with roman numerals. NCTs have been put in parentheses (other interpretations are possible). Which chord could be considered an example of secondary mode mixture?

Bach, "Herr Jesu Christ, wahr'r Mensch und Gott"

C:

2. Label the chords and NCTs. Circle the roman numerals of any borrowed chords.

Schumann, "Ich grolle nicht"

3. Label the chords, circling the roman numerals of any borrowed chords. Label the cadence type.

Brahms, Symphony No. 3, Op. 90, II

4. This excerpt modulates from D to B♭ by means of a common-chord modulation. Label all chords with roman numerals.

Beethoven, Sonata Op. 10, No. 3, IV

5. This excerpt modulates from A♭ to some other key and then back to A♭. Label all chords and NCTs.

Schubert, Impromptu Op. 90, No. 1

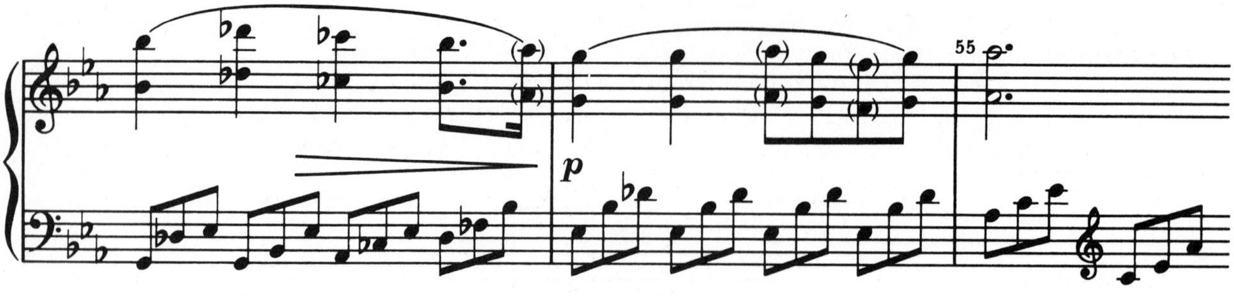

D. Part writing. Analyze the chords implied by the soprano/bass framework. Then fill in alto and tenor parts. Be sure to use the specified mode mixture.

1. Include a $\text{ii}^{\varnothing 6}_{5}$.

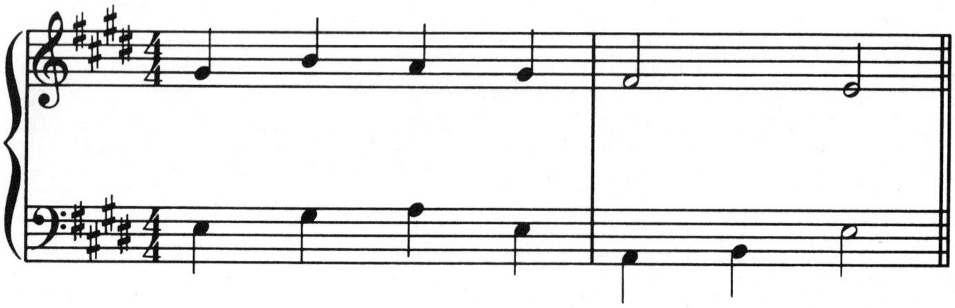

2. Include a iv^{6} and a $\text{ii}^{\varnothing 4}_{3}$.

E. The first two phrases of a chorale melody are given below. A bass line is included for the first phrase. Complete the four-part texture, including in the second phrase a modulation to B♭ and a borrowed iv^6 chord. Label all chords and circle the roman numeral of the borrowed chord. Activate the texture with NCTs and/or arpeggiations.

F. Analyze the harmonies specified by the following figured bass, and then make an arrangement for SATB chorus. This passage does modulate.

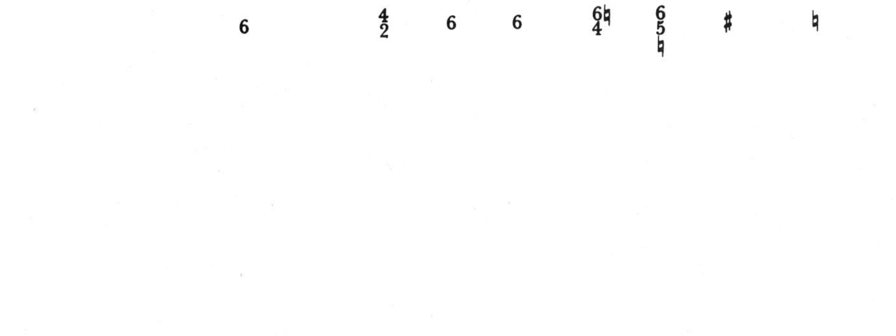

G. Arrange the first modulation below for SAB chorus and the second one for SATB chorus. Activate the textures with NCTs and/or arpeggiations. Arrange the metric and rhythmic structure so that the last chord comes on a strong beat. Label chords and NCTs.

1. D: I V I^6 vi iv^6

F: ii^6 V^4_2 I^6 II^6_5 I^6_4 V I

2. F: I vii^{o6}_5 I^6 V^6_5 I vii^{o4}_3/IV iv^6

b♭: i^6 iv i^6_4 V I

H. Use the framework below as the basis for the beginning of a passage that starts in F major and modulates to D♭ major by means of mode mixture. Score for piano or for some combination of instruments in your class.

CHAPTER TWENTY-TWO

THE NEAPOLITAN CHORD

EXERCISE 22-1

A. Label each chord. Include inversions, if appropriate.

F: ___ c: ___ D: ___ b♭: ___ e: ___

D: ___ E: ___ d: ___ f♯: ___ A♭: ___

B. Notate each chord. Include key signatures.

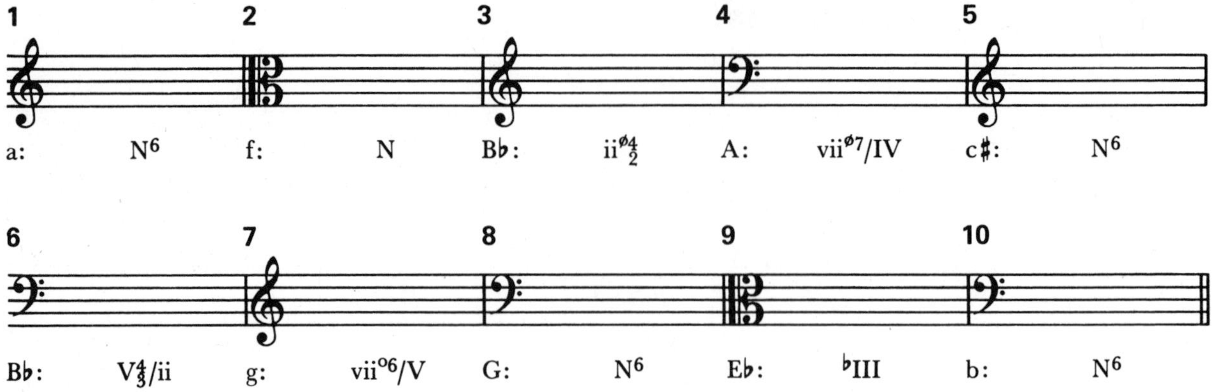

C. Analysis.

1. Label chords and NCTs.

Chopin, Prelude Op. 28, No. 20

2. Label the chords in this excerpt.

Beethoven, Sonata Op. 27, No. 2, I

c♯:

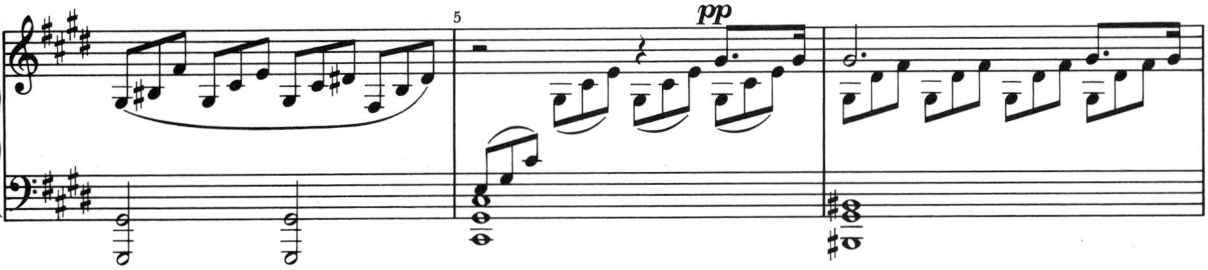

3. At this point in Schubert's famous "Erlkönig," the evil personality of the title character is finally expressed, with the help of the Neapolitan triad. Label the chords.

Schubert, "Erlkönig," Op. 1

d:

4. At the end of the song, the father's frantic ride comes to an end, and we hear the Neapolitan again. Label the chords.

Schubert, "Erlkönig," Op. 1

D. For each exercise, provide the correct key signature and notate the specified chords preceding and following the N^6. Use the given three- or four-part texture in each case.

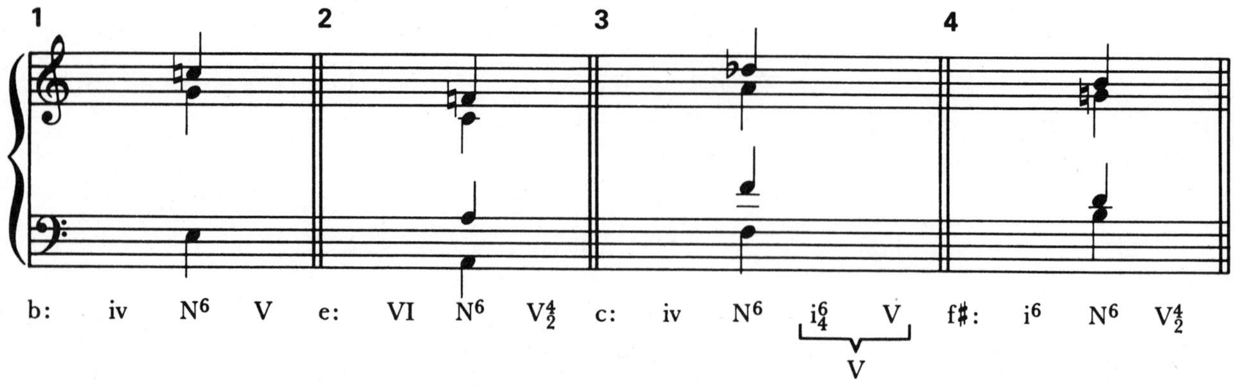

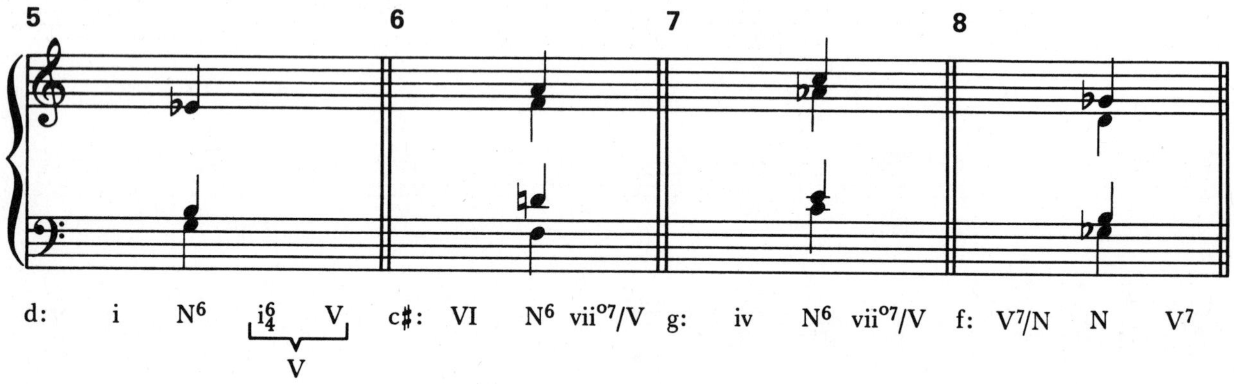

E. Analyze the harmonies implied by the soprano/bass framework. Then fill in inner voices to make a four-part texture. Each exercise should contain a Neapolitan chord.

3

c:

F. Analyze the chords specified by this figured bass, and then make an arrangement for SATB chorus.

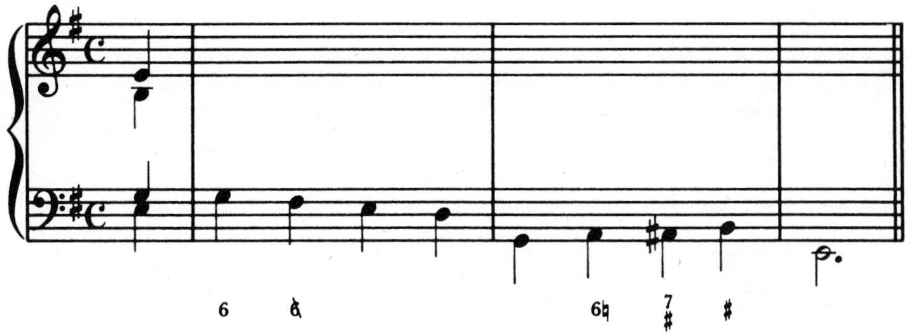

G. Make settings of the following progressions for three or four parts, as specified. Arrange the rhythmic/metric scheme so that the final chord of each progression comes on a strong beat. Activate the texture with arpeggiations and/or NCTs.

1. (4 parts) g: i V i^6 i VI V$^4_2$/N N^6 vii^{o7}/V i$^6_4$ V i

2. (3 parts) e: i V$^4_2$/iv iv^6 i$^6_4$ N^6 V$^4_2$ i^6 vii^{o6} i

3. (4 parts) E♭: I I^6 vi ii V I^6
d: N^6 vii^{o7}/V i$^6_4$ V^7 i

4. (3 parts) b: i V VI i^6 N^6
G: IV^6 V$^6_5$ I V I

H. Use the framework below as the first phrase of a three-phrase excerpt having the following structure:

b: HC ⇝ f♯: HC PAC

Phrase 2 modulates to f♯ minor. Phrase 3 remains in f♯ minor and contains a Neapolitan triad. After completing the framework, make a more elaborate version for piano or for some combination of instruments in your class.

I. Make a setting of the following text or of some text of your choice for three-part chorus. Include in your setting examples of the following:

Neapolitan triad

Mode mixture

Common-chord modulation

Your composition should begin and end in the same key. Be sure to include a harmonic analysis.

A storm of white petals,
Buds throwing open baby fists
Into hands of broad flowers.

—From "The Year," in *Cornhuskers* by Carl Sandburg, copyright 1918 by Holt, Rinehart and Winston, Inc.; renewed 1946 by Carl Sandburg. Reprinted by permission of Harcourt Brace Jovanovich, Inc.

CHAPTER TWENTY-THREE

AUGMENTED SIXTH CHORDS 1

EXERCISE 23-1

A. Label each chord, using inversion symbols where appropriate.

c♯: ___ b: ___ f: ___ E♭: ___ D: ___

E: ___ D♭: ___ a: ___ g: ___ F: ___

B. Notate each chord in close position. Augmented sixth chords should be in their customary bass position ($\flat\hat{6}$ in the bass). Include key signatures.

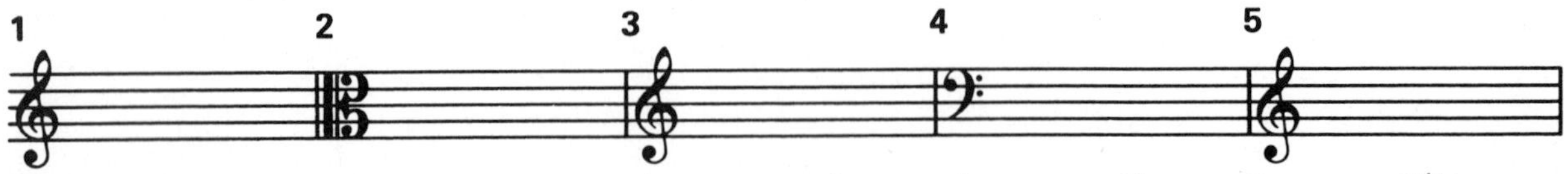

B♭: Fr^{+6} d: N^{6} b♭: Ger^{+6} A♭: It^{+6} B: ii$^{ø6}_{5}$

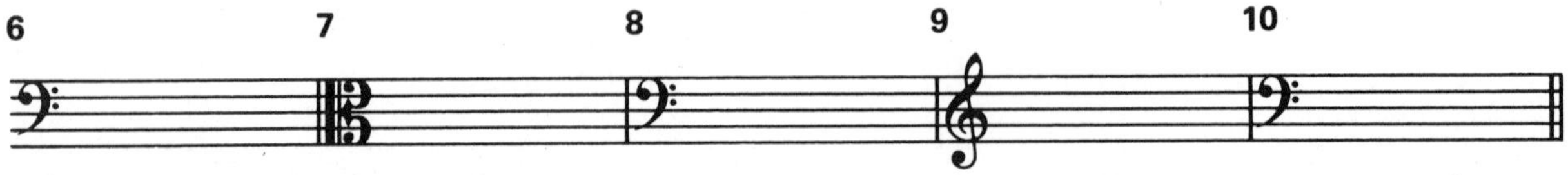

f♯: It^{+6} A: Ger^{+6} c: Fr^{+6} G: vii^{o7}/vi e: Ger^{+6}

C. Label the chords in each example below. Also, discuss the details of the resolution of each augmented sixth chord. Do $\sharp\hat{4}$ and $\flat\hat{6}$ follow their expected resolutions to $\hat{5}$? How are parallel 5ths avoided in the Ger^{+6} resolution(s)?

1. Measures 2-5 of this excerpt are in d minor, although the key of VI (B♭) is strongly tonicized in mm. 2-3 (the second chord in m. 2 should be analyzed as a secondary function of VI). Common-chord modulations to two other keys occur in mm. 5-11.

Schumann, "Sehnsucht," Op. 51, No. 1

Thrä - ne mir fällt; wohl leuch - tet die Fer - ne mit gol - de-nem Licht, doch
hält mich der Nord, ich er - rei - che sie nicht. O die Schran - ken so eng, und die
Welt so weit,

2. This excerpt begins in C major and modulates. Where is there a 9-8 suspension?

Haydn, Quartet Op. 74, No. 3, II

3. This excerpt begins and ends in g minor, but it contains modulations to two other keys (or tonicizations of two other chords). How do those keys relate to the "parent" tonality of g minor?

Schumann, "Die beiden Grenadiere," Op. 49, No. 1

4. The slow tempo of this theme allows some measures to contain several chords. In the first measure, for instance, each bass note is harmonized by a new chord, with the exception of the B2. Discuss the various uses of the pitch class G♯/A♭ in this excerpt.

Beethoven, Trio Op. 9, No. 3, II

5
pp
rinf.
(pp)
10
sf

D. Supply the missing voices for each fragment below. All are four-part textures.

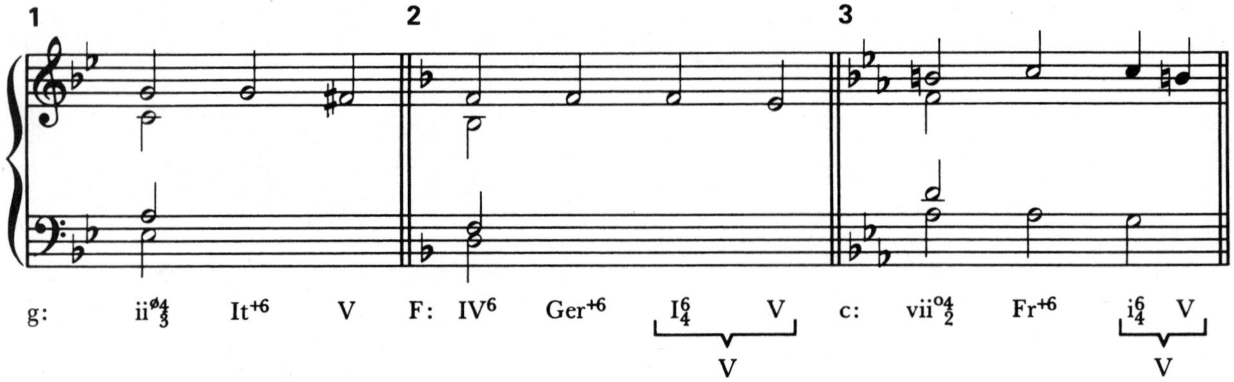

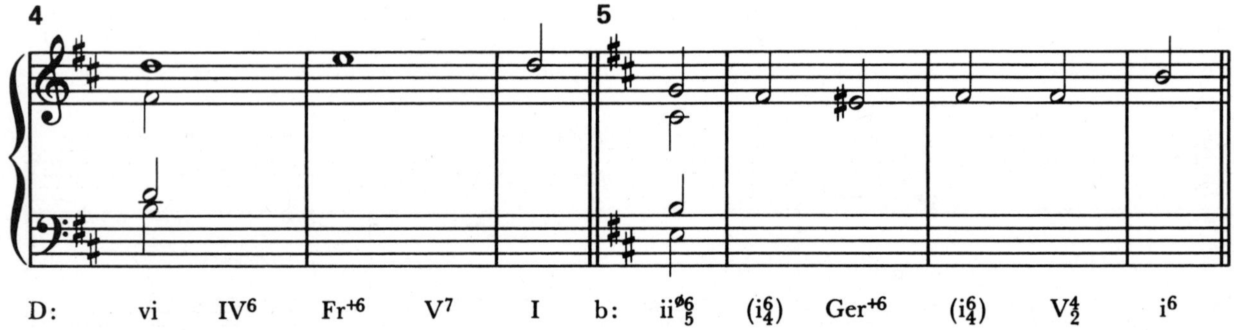

E. Complete these harmonizations, adding one or two inner voices, as specified.

F. Analyze the harmonies specified by this figured bass, and then make an arrangement for SATB chorus.

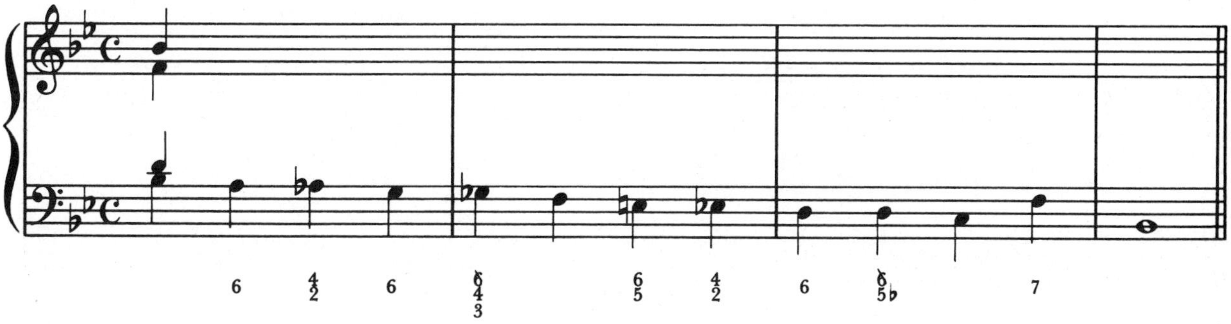

G. Analyze the harmonies implied by this soprano/bass framework, being sure to include an It^{+6}. Then fill in the inner voices, following good voice-leading procedures. There are no NCTs in the bass and soprano lines.

H. Given below are mm. 1-2 of a four-measure phrase. Continue the passage to make a period (parallel or contrasting) that ends with a PAC in the key of the dominant. Include an augmented sixth chord.

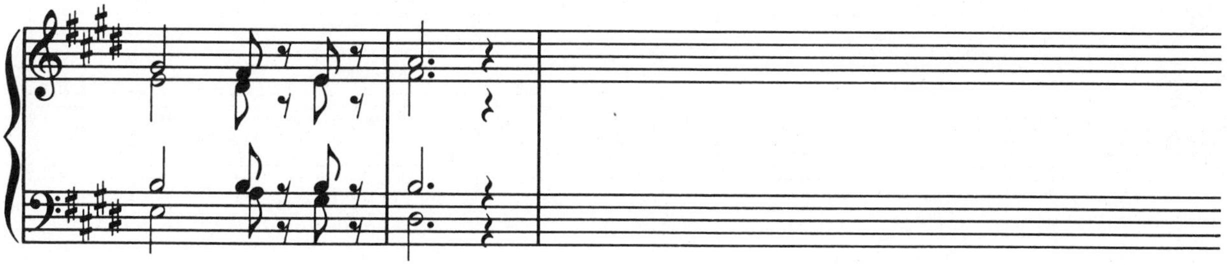

I. Make a setting of the following text or of some text of your choice for three-part chorus. Include in your setting examples of the following:

Neapolitan triad

Mode mixture

Secondary function

Augmented sixth chord

Remember to include tempo indication and dynamic markings.

Two roads diverged in a wood, and I –
I took the one less traveled by,
And that has made all the difference.

CHAPTER TWENTY-FOUR

AUGMENTED SIXTH CHORDS 2

EXERCISE 24-1

A. Label the chords in the keys indicated.

1 2 3 4 5

g: ___ ___ b: ___ ___ A♭: ___ ___ ___ G: ___ ___ f♯: ___ ___

6 7 8 9 10

f: ___ ___ d: ___ ___ E♭: ___ ___ ___ E: ___ ___ B♭: ___ ___

B. Analysis.

1. Label the chords in this example. Measures 10-12 could be analyzed in terms of secondary functions or as a modulation.

Tchaikovsky, "The Nurse's Tale," Op. 39, No. 19

2. In a number of his works Scriabin used the chord found at the end of the first measure. Label the chords.

Scriabin, *Tragic Poem,* Op. 34

3. This excerpt will give you practice with both alto and tenor clefs. Label all chords and NCTs.

Schubert, String Trio D. 581

4. This example begins in A and modulates. Label the chords.

Schumann, "Novellette," Op. 21, No. 7 (simplified texture)

f♯:

CHAPTER TWENTY-FIVE

ENHARMONIC SPELLINGS AND ENHARMONIC MODULATIONS

EXERCISE 25-1

A. Analyze the given chord. Then show any possible enharmonic reinterpretation(s) of that chord, keeping the same key signature. The enharmonic reinterpretation should involve a new key, not just an enharmonically equivalent key (like g♯ and a♭). Number 1 is supplied as an example.

1 2 3

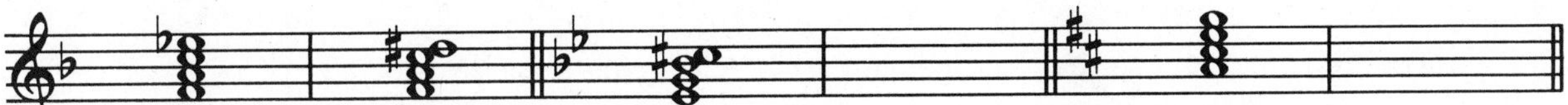

F: V^7/IV = A: Ger+6 g: ______ = ______ D: ______ = ______

4 5

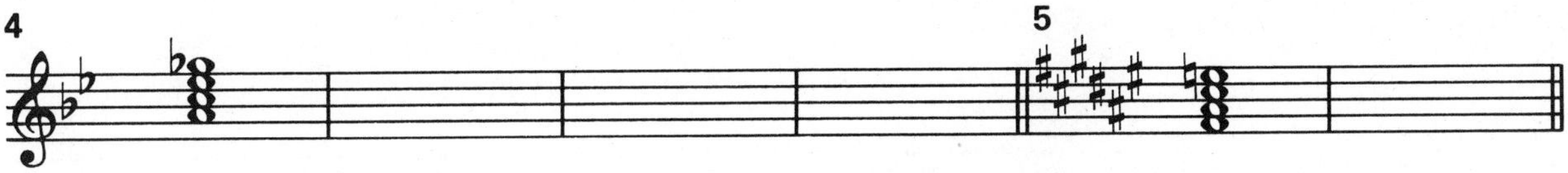

B♭: ______ = ______ = ______ = ______ F♯: ______ = ______

B. Each of the following short passages contains an enharmonic modulation. Analyze each passage after playing it slowly at the piano and listening for the point of modulation. Do not try to analyze these passages without hearing them.

1

2

3

C. Compose short passages similar to those in Part B. The given chord is to serve as the common chord in an enharmonic modulation. (Hint: As you sketch out your progression, notate the given chord first. Then find satisfactory ways to lead into and away from that chord.)

1. G to B. Common chord: V^7/IV in G.

2. b to B♭. Common chord: vii^{o7}/iv in b.

3. B♭ to E. Common chord: vii$^{\circ 6}_{5}$ on B♭.

4. E to F. Common chord: Ger^{+6} in E.

D. Analysis. Be sure to play as much as you can of each excerpt.

1. This excerpt begins in g minor. Label all the chords.

Beethoven, Sonata Op. 13, I

2. This passage modulates from f♯ minor to A♭ major by way of E major. The bass notes are found above the "*Ped.*" markings—the other notes in the bass clef are arpeggiations into inner voices. Label all of the chords, including common chords for both modulations.

Chopin, Nocturne Op. 27, No. 1

3. The next excerpt is quite challenging. Label both chords and NCTs. You might find it helpful to label the chords with pop symbols before assigning roman numerals.

Haydn, Quartet Op. 76, No. 6, II

4. This excerpt begins in B major and ends in E major, but there are modulations to B♭ and D♭ along the way. Label all of the chords, and analyze common chords for each modulation.

Schubert, Piano Sonata in B♭, D. 960, I

come sopra
f
155
p
cresc.
ff
p
160
tranquillo
pp
pp
165
p

5. This excerpt begins and ends in B♭, but it hints at the key of E along the way. Analyze the reference to E as a modulation, labeling common chords going into E and returning to B♭.

Schumann, "Am leuchtenden Sommermorgen," Op. 48, No. 12

E. Use mm. 31-34 of Part D, number 3, as the first phrase of an eight-measure parallel period. The second phrase should include an enharmonic modulation to a foreign key.

F. Compose the beginning of a song with piano accompaniment, using a text of your choice. Include two enharmonic modulations, one of them using a Ger^{+6} chord, the other a diminished seventh chord.

CHAPTER TWENTY-SIX

FURTHER ELEMENTS OF THE HARMONIC VOCABULARY

EXERCISE 26-1

A. In each fragment below, analyze the given chord. Then notate the specified chord in such a way that it leads smoothly into the given chord with acceptable voice leading. Some of the problems use a five-part texture for simpler voice leading.

D: IV^{M9} ___ E♭: (ct^{o7}) ___ b: $V^{7\,subs.}_{6th}$ ___ A: V^{+7} ___

F♯: (ct^{o7}) ___ B♭: V^{+6}/IV ___ E: $ii^{\o 4}_{3}$ ___ g: V^{9} ___

B. Compose four short passages for piano, each one making use of a different progression from Part A. The half-note durations do not need to be retained, but use the same voice leading.

C. Analysis. Throughout this section highlight (using arrows or whatever is convenient) any occurrences of the chords discussed in this chapter.

1. This excerpt is in e minor throughout, with the exception of a short modulation to the relative major. Label all chords and NCTs.

Bach, "Jesu, meine Freude"

2. Label chords and NCTs.

Schumann, *Humoresque,* Op. 20

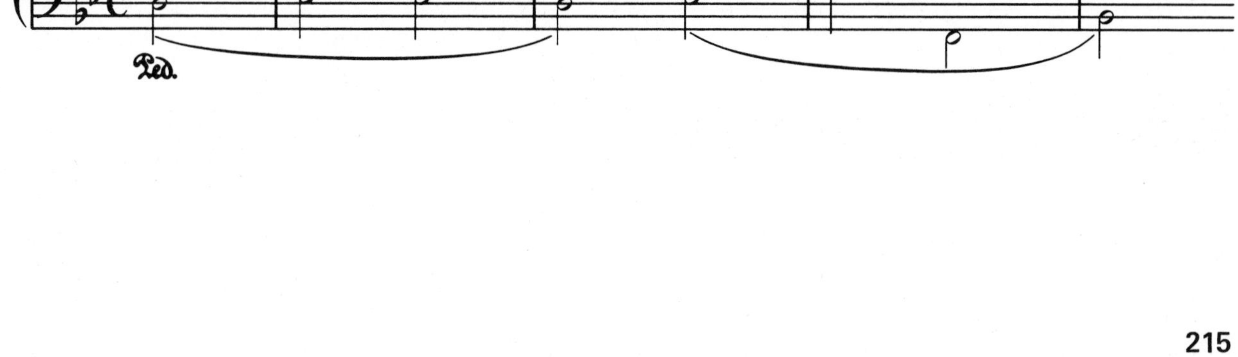

3. Label chords and NCTs. There are no transposing instruments in this excerpt, but there is a set of parallel 5ths—see whether you can find them.

Beethoven, *The Creatures of Prometheus,* Op. 43, Overture

4. Harmonic sequences occupy most of this excerpt. Find the two sequences, and bracket each occurrence of the sequential patterns. If it is possible to do so, label the chords in the sequences with roman numerals, perhaps in terms of shifting tonalities. Discuss briefly the large-scale harmonic/melodic function of each sequence—in other words, just what does each sequence accomplish harmonically and melodically?

Schumann, "Die Löwenbraut," Op. 31, No. 1

5. This familiar excerpt is easier to listen to than to analyze. The transpositions do not make the analysis any easier—clarinets in A and horns in F—nor do the four clefs in use. Do your best with the score (after all, conductors face this sort of problem every day), then check your work with the piano arrangement that follows the excerpt.

Tchaikovsky, Symphony No. 6, Op. 74, I

incalzando
ritenuto
95
Clar. I in A
Clar. II in A
Bsn.
Hn. in F
Vl. I
Vl. II
con sordini
Vla.
con sordini
Vc.
D.B.

6. Label with roman numerals the two chords in this excerpt that are the most important structurally. The other chords are simultaneities connecting the structural chords. Label their roots. If any of these chords imply fleeting tonicizations, indicate this with roman numerals. The chord in m. 2 could be heard as a g triad with raised *and* lowered 5th (G/B♭/D♭/D♯), since the E♭ ascends chromatically to E, as we would expect D♯ to do. Find another chord in this passage that could be interpreted similarly.

Wagner, *Siegfried,* Act I (piano-vocal score)

7. In some ways this excerpt pushes traditional harmony toward its limits, especially through its disregard for conventional resolutions of dissonance. Nevertheless, the entire passage can be analyzed reasonably well in traditional terms. Label all of the chords. Which portion of the excerpt is the most unconventional in terms of dissonance treatment?

Grieg, "The Mountain Maid," Op. 67, No. 2

CHAPTER TWENTY-SEVEN

TONAL HARMONY IN THE LATE NINETEENTH CENTURY

EXERCISE 27-1

A. Examine the first twenty-five measures of the opening of *Tannhäuser,* given below, and do the following:

1. The opening eight measures show rather traditional harmonic function. Analyze these measures, using roman numerals (do all work on the music).
2. The following eight measures, which may also be analyzed with roman numerals, show less traditional harmonic movement. Cite at least three instances in which this is true (show measure number).

   a. ______________________________

   b. ______________________________

   c. ______________________________

3. Analyze the sequence that begins at m. 17 and continues through m. 21.

m. 17	m. 18	m. 19	m. 20	m. 21

Use pop symbols, roman numerals, or a mixture of both, whichever seems appropriate. Circle those chords which are most strongly tonicized. How is such tonicization accomplished?

Wagner, *Tannhäuser,* Prelude to Act I (piano reduction)

10
15
20
25

B. Analyze the following chromatic sequences; then continue each as indicated.

1

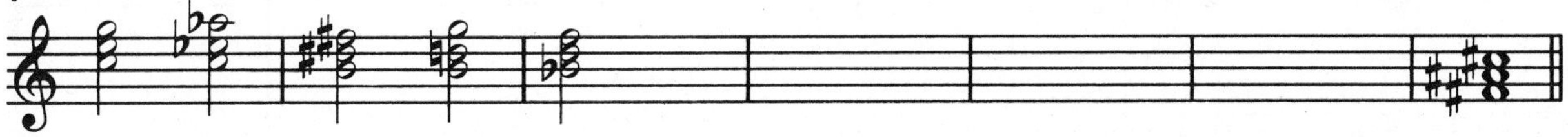

2

3

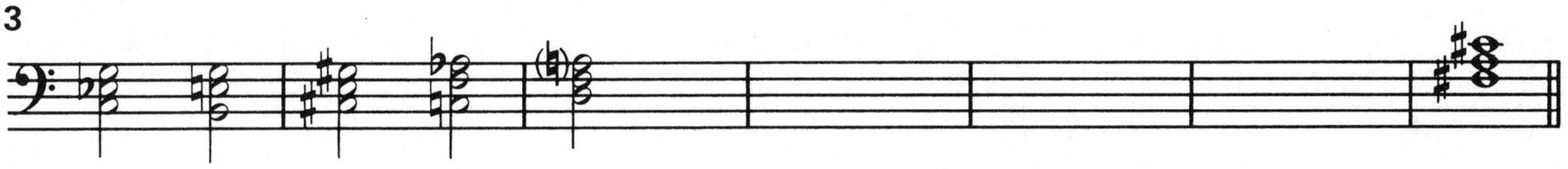

4

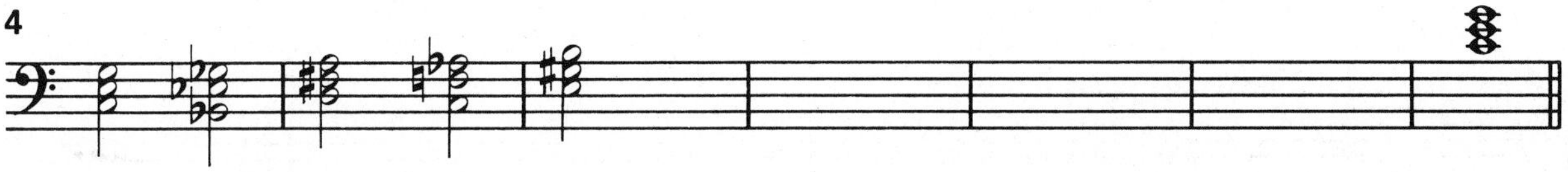

Select one of the above sequence patterns to serve as the basis for a piano composition. You may wish to create a melody over the background of block chords, or perhaps modify the texture of the harmonies themselves. Nonessential or embellishing chords may be inserted within the sequence for the purpose of color.

C. Continue the following sequences as indicated. Then select one to serve as the harmonic basis for a piano or vocal composition in the style of one of the post-romantic composers studied. Strive for contrapuntal interest and smooth voice leading.

1

2

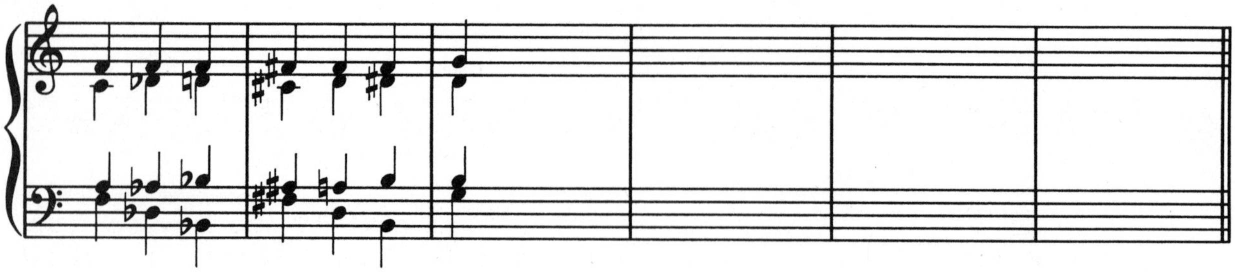

3

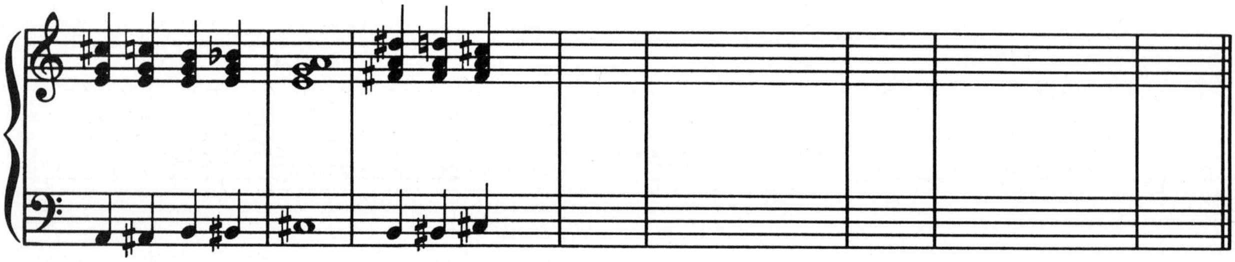

D. Examine the following excerpt.

1. The opening key is designated as E major. What is interesting about the structure of the scale which forms the basis for mm. 2 and 3? ________

____

____

2. Provide roman numeral analysis for m. 2. ____________________
In what way does the music in mm. 10-11 suggest more traditional treatment of tonality? ____________________

____

3. Describe the modulatory procedure which takes place in mm. 12-13.

____

____

4. Name the key introduced in m. 14. ____________________

What is its relationship to the opening key? ____________________

5. Name two other keys hinted at between mm. 1 and 14. ____________

and ____________ These keys represent what relationship to each other and to the opening key? ____________________

Wolf, "Die ihr schwebet um diese Palmen"

10
es schlum - mert mein Kind.
f
mf
f
Ihr Pal - men
15
von Beth - le - hem im
f
p

E. **1.** Is there a clear tonal center in the opening five bars of the following excerpt? If so, what is it, and how is it defined? ______________

____

____

2. Using pop symbols, name the two sonorities found in mm. 6 and 7.

____________ and ____________ In what way could these chords be said to suggest functional harmony in the key of D major which ultimately concludes the excerpt, as well as the piece? ___________

____

3. What roman numerals are used in mm. 9-12 to prepare the cadence in D major?

m. 9	m. 10	m. 11	m. 12

Wolf, "Verschwiegene Liebe"

5
in den Glanz hin - ein, wer mag sie er - ra - ten, wer
p
hol - te sie ein? Ge -
rit.
pp rit.
a tempo
p 10
pp
dan - ken sich wie - gen, die Nacht ist ver-schwie - gen, Ge -
a tempo
p
pp

dan - - ken sind frei. Er -
p
mf
f
p

F. **1.** The following excerpt begins and ends in E major. What is unusual about the manner in which the key is established in mm. 1-4?

____

____

____

2. Label on the music the harmonies found in mm. 5-12. Use pop symbols for your analysis.

3. What five-chord succession within the preceding section represents an "omnibus" fragment? ______________________

4. In what way is the approach to the closing E major harmony unusual?

____

____

5. By what means does Fauré make it convincing, nonetheless?

____

____

____

Fauré, "Chanson d'Amour," Op. 27, No. 1 (mm. 10-22)

poco a poco (,) cresc.
dis, O ma re - belle, ô mon cher an - ge,
cresc.
20 f (,) (,) p
Mon en - fer et mon pa - ra - dis! J'ai - me tes yeux
mf
p

G. The first ten measures of *Reverie* may be analyzed with traditional roman numerals (if you watch out for enharmonic respellings). Do so; then comment on reasons for the rather contemporary sound of the piece.

D. Payne, *Reverie*

H. **1.** In the *Siegfried* excerpt, analyze one essential harmony for each of the first eleven measures of the excerpt.

m. 1 m. 2 m. 3 m. 4 m. 5 m. 6 m. 7 m. 8 m. 9 m. 10 m. 11

2. Name at least three keys (including the first one) which are established throughout the course of this excerpt. Show measure numbers.

______________ ______________ ______________

3. Show two instances in which modulation is effected by deceptive resolution, either of chords or of single pitches. Describe the process

that takes place. ____

Wagner, *Siegfried* (Act III, Scene 3)

(feurig, doch zart)
wig zu dei - nem Heil! O Sieg - fried, Herr - li - cher! Hort der
poco f
p
sf
Welt! Le - ben der Er - de, la - chen - der
Held! Lass', ach, lass'! Las - se von mir! Na he mir nicht mit der
cresc.

I. **1.** What is unusual about the treatment of tonality in the opening four measures? ______________________________

____

____

2. Describe the non-traditional treatment of the dominant seventh sonority in mm. 5-9 of the excerpt. ______________________________

____

____

3. In what way is the musical style significantly influenced by the treatment of nonharmonic material? Consider both single tones and vertical sonorities. ______________________________

____

____

____

Franck, *Prelude, Aria, and Finale for Piano* (Prelude)

J. **1.** Show roman numeral analysis in mm. 1-16. Do all work on the music. Note the absence of a clear dominant-tonic cadence anywhere in the excerpt. Locate illustrations of avoided tonic cadence, and describe the manner in which this is accomplished. ______________________

____

____

2. What other procedures mark this as a late Romantic work? __________

____

____

____

Brahms, Symphony No. 1, Op. 68, II (piano reduction)

K. The following excerpt is taken from the *Barcarolle,* Op. 17, No. 6, by Richard Strauss (mm. 21-30).

1. What key is implied by the melody in the opening four bars? ________

2. What means does Strauss employ to negate that tonal implication, and indeed, any clear tonal implication? ________________________

____

____

____

3. Show the underlying harmonic structure of mm. 25-29, using pop symbols.

m. 25	m. 26	m. 27	m. 28	m. 29

4. Within the passage shown above, locate and describe at least three examples of deceptive resolution which serve to make the chord succession convincing.

a. ________________________________

b. ________________________________

c. ________________________________

R. Strauss, *Barcarolle,* Op. 17, No. 6

seh' ich das saü - len - ge - tra - ge - ne Dach,
25
dim.
poco calando
und das flim - mern - de Licht am Al - ta - ne kün - det mir, dass die Ge -
dim.
lieb - te noch wach.
30 a tempo
Flie - ge, mein
a tempo
p

CHAPTER TWENTY-EIGHT

AN INTRODUCTION TO TWENTIETH-CENTURY PRACTICES

EXERCISE 28-1

A. Add the appropriate accidentals (or delete the appropriate notes) to create the type of scale asked for.

Mixolydian | Pentatonic

♯4, ♭7 | Phrygian

Whole tone | Locrian

B. Using the pentatonic scale of B♭-C-D-F-G, compose five brief melodies, each of which in turn establishes a different one of the above pitches as tonic. (Hint: D is tough. Why?)

1

2

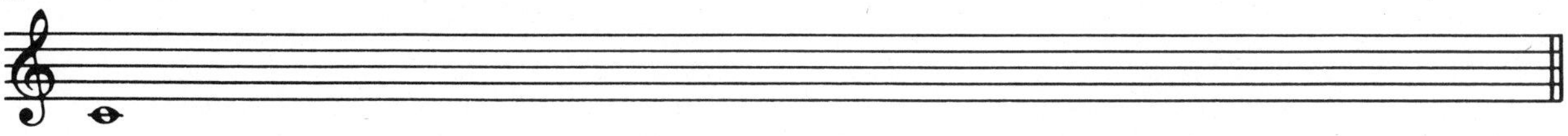

3

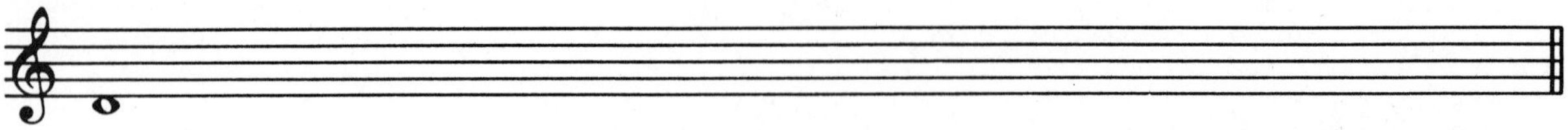

4

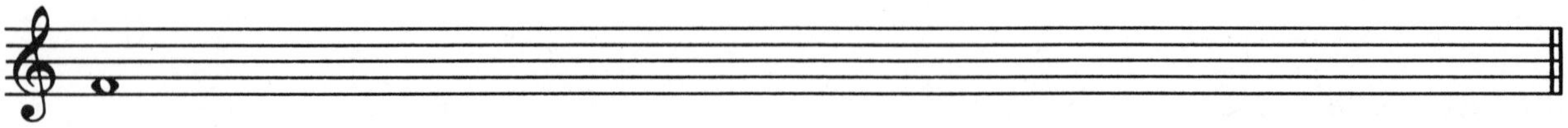

5

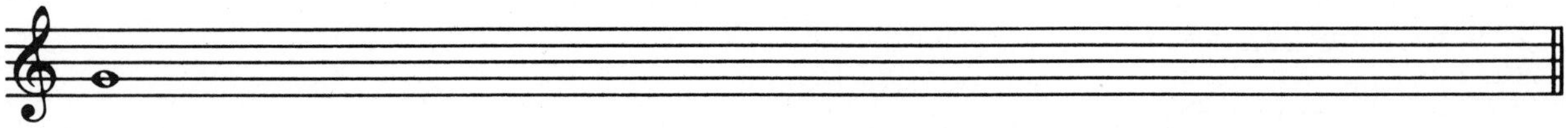

C. **1.** All the modes contain a perfect fifth from $\hat{1}$ up to $\hat{5}$ except the

________ .

2. The three modes that are essentially *minor* in quality are the

________ , ________ , and ________ .

3. The modal scales that contain a leading tone are the

________ and ________ .

4. The $\hat{1}$-$\hat{4}$ tetrachord in the Mixolydian scale matches that of the

________ scale.

5. Likewise, the opening tetrachord of the Aeolian and ______________ scale is the same.

6. Those scales containing a major sixth from $\hat{1}$ up to $\hat{6}$ are the

________ , ________ , ________ , and ________ .

7. Name the interval from $\hat{1}$ up to $\hat{4}$ in a Lydian scale. ______________

8. Name the interval from $\hat{4}$ up to $\hat{7}$ in a Mixolydian scale. ____________

D. Identify the scale that forms the basis for the following melodies:

1 **Moderately**

1. ____________________

2

2. ____________________

3

3. ____________________

E. Identify the scale used in the following passages:

1 **Allegretto**

1. ____________________

2

2. ______________________

3

3. ______________________

F. The following examples represent three versions of the principal tune from Debussy's "Fêtes." For each, identify the mode or scale being used.

Debussy, "Fêtes," from *Nocturnes* (piano reduction)

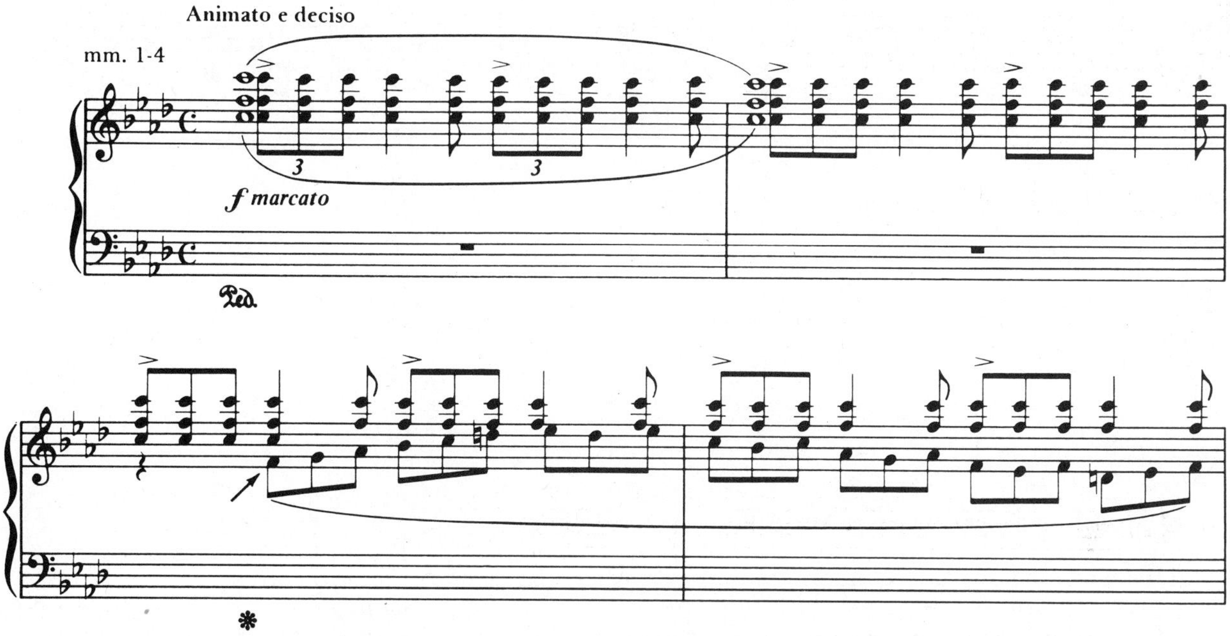

scale: ______________________________

scale: ______________________________

mm. 29-32

scale: ______________________________

G. Compose pieces according to the following specifications:

1. Create a melody that contains no intervals other than major or minor 3rds. Use rhythmic interest to keep your melody from sounding like a series of arpeggios. You may find it interesting to analyze the pitches that comprise your finished melody and see if a particular scale pattern emerges.

2. Create a two-voice composition based on a whole-tone scale. You might wish to create a symmetrical relationship between the two voices, or perhaps treat them imitatively. If your composition is for piano, experiment with the wide range of the keyboard.

H. Describe the types of vertical sonorities found in the following examples:

1

1. ______________________________

2

2. ______________________________

3

3. ______________________________

4

4. ______________________________

I. Complete the following passages using *strict* parallelism. That is, harmonize each melody note with a chord scored exactly like the preceding one in terms of vertical intervals. Try playing these at the keyboard.

1

2

3

4

5

6

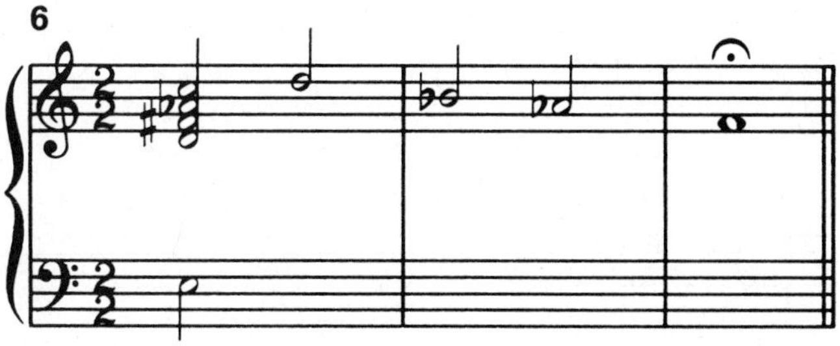

7

8

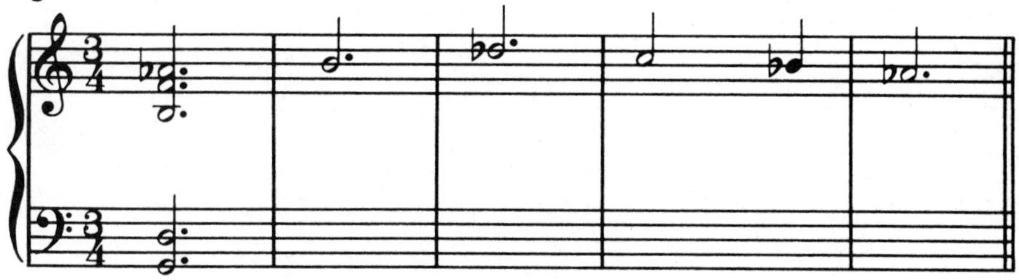

9

10

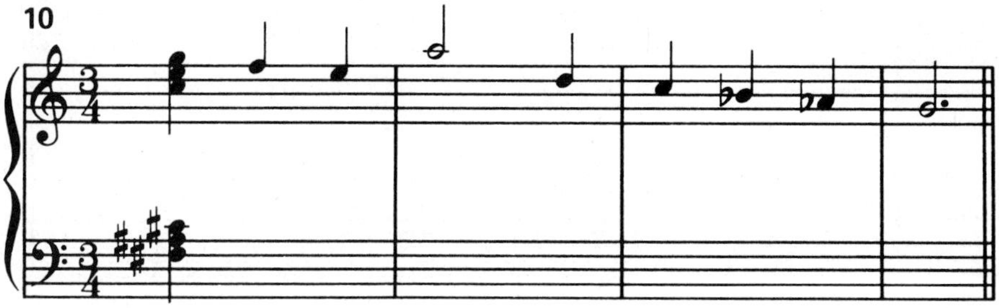

J. Devise completions for the following passages. Include both black and white keys in your solution. Try to maintain stylistic consistency.

1

2

3

K. Compose a brief work for piano employing tall chords, including a few eleventhths and thirteenths, in a basically non-tonal context. Include some examples of strict planing.

L. Complete the following passages, using the triad type indicated for each hand. Continue the scoring suggested by the first polychord, using the given outer parts consistently as either roots, 3rds, or 5ths of the sonority.

1

2

3

4

5

M. Comment on the stylistic features of the following excerpts. Consider rhythm, texture, pitch choice, and treatment of tonality.

1

1. ____

____

____

2 Moderato ♩ = 92

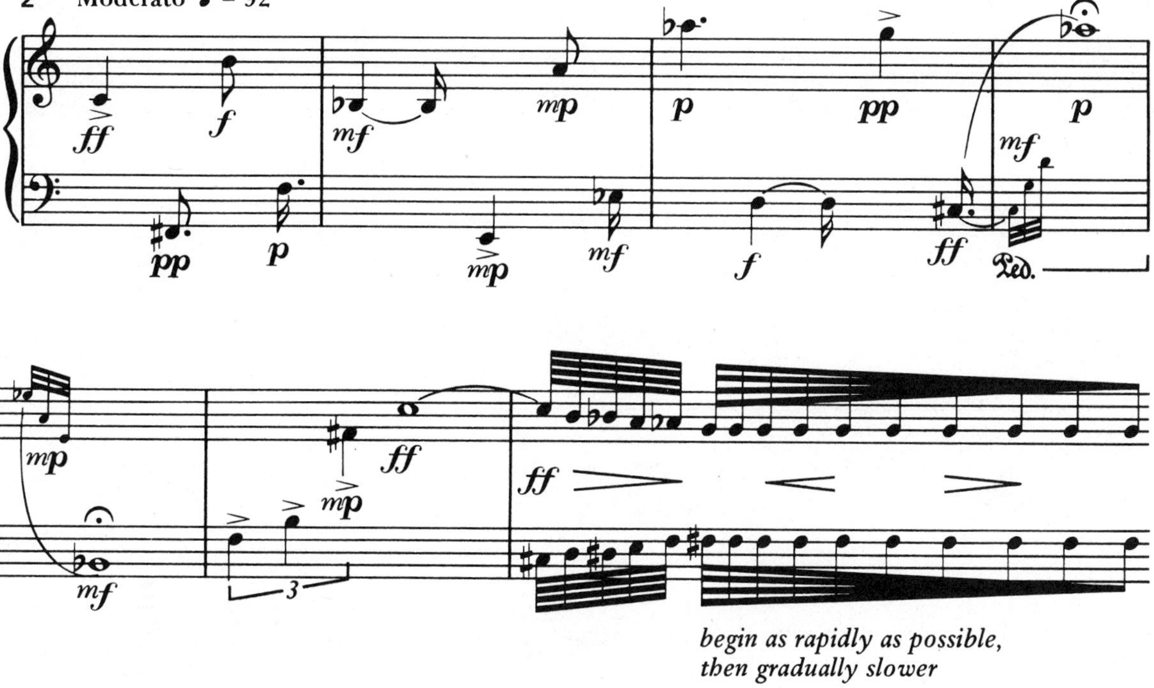

2. ____

____

____

____

Stravinsky, "Danse russe," from *Petrouchka* (piano reduction)

3

3. ____

____

Stravinsky, "Danse de la foire," from *Petrouchka* (piano reduction)

4

Used by permission of Edward B. Marks Music Co.

4. ____

____

N. Examine the following étude.

1. What is interesting about the relationship of the left and right hands throughout the piece? ______________________________

____

____

2. What is the opening key of the piece? ______________________________

3. What scale is employed in measures 11-20? ______________________________

4. In what sense is this scale pattern "violated" in measures 17 and 18?

____

5. In what way does the ending of the piece refer back to the middle section? ______________________________

6. How would you describe the overall form of the piece? ______________________________

____

D. Payne, *Étude*

f
20
molto ritard.
25

O. Notate the pitches of the following trichords, as indicated. Where necessary, rearrange each set in *normal order.* For each trichord, give vector analysis.

[3,4,9] ____________ [6,9,2] ____________

[2,4,9] ____________ [9,10,4] ____________

[1,8,11] ____________ [0,5,10] ____________

P. For each of the following sonorities, provide (1) vector analysis, and (2) name of chord, if appropriate (i.e., polychord, mystic chord, etc.).

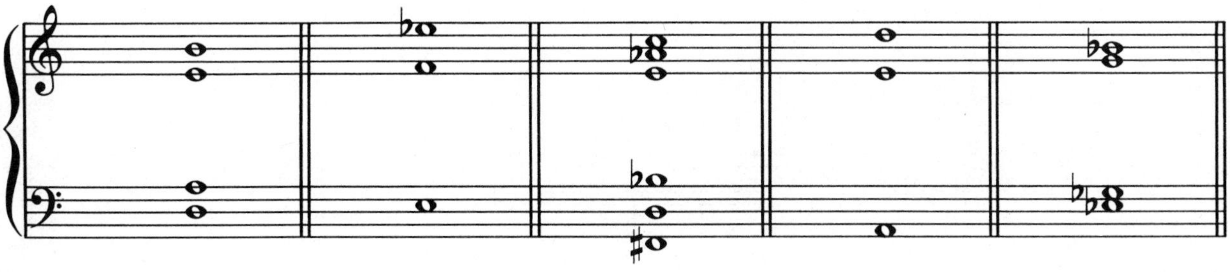

Q. **1.** Analyze the intervals in the following twelve-tone set (row). Does any relation exist between the first and second halves (hexachords)? Then mirror (invert) the row a m6 higher. Finally, retrograde it a M6 lower.

(P^0)

I↑m6

(I^8)

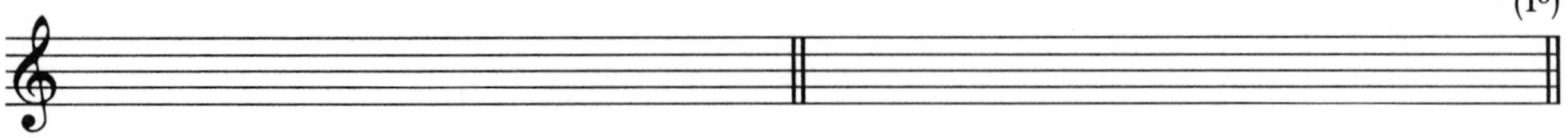

R↓M6

(R^3)

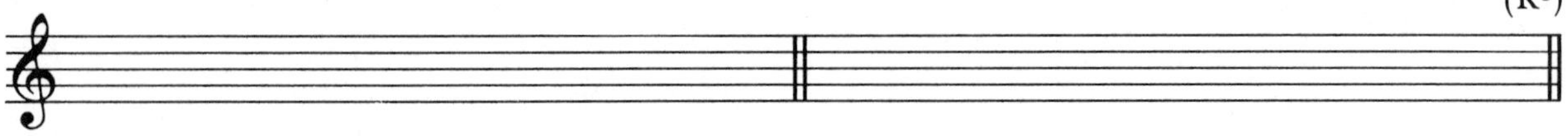

2. Mirror (or invert) the intervals.

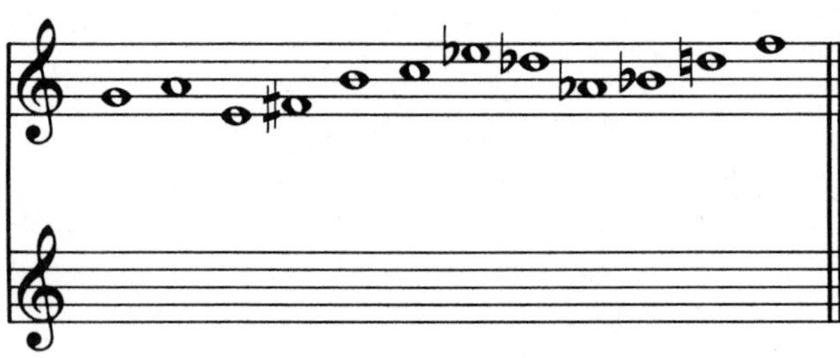

3. Transpose a m3 higher.

4. Transpose the retrograde a P4 higher.

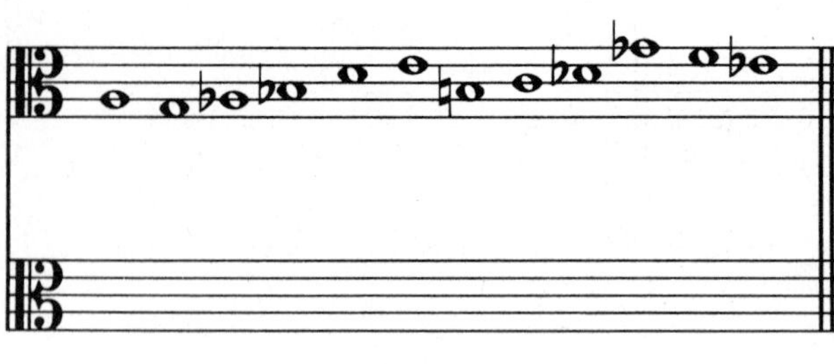

5. Mirror (or invert) the retrograde.

6. Which of the above is not a twelve-tone row? ____________________

R. The row shown below provides the basis for Berg's *Lyric Suite.* Complete the Babbitt Square, showing the various set forms and their transpositions. Number the prime and inversion forms in ascending order (chromatically) above the starting pitch. What is interesting about the original pitch set?

In the space provided, indicate prime forms for each of the trichords comprising the row. What does this reveal? ______________________________

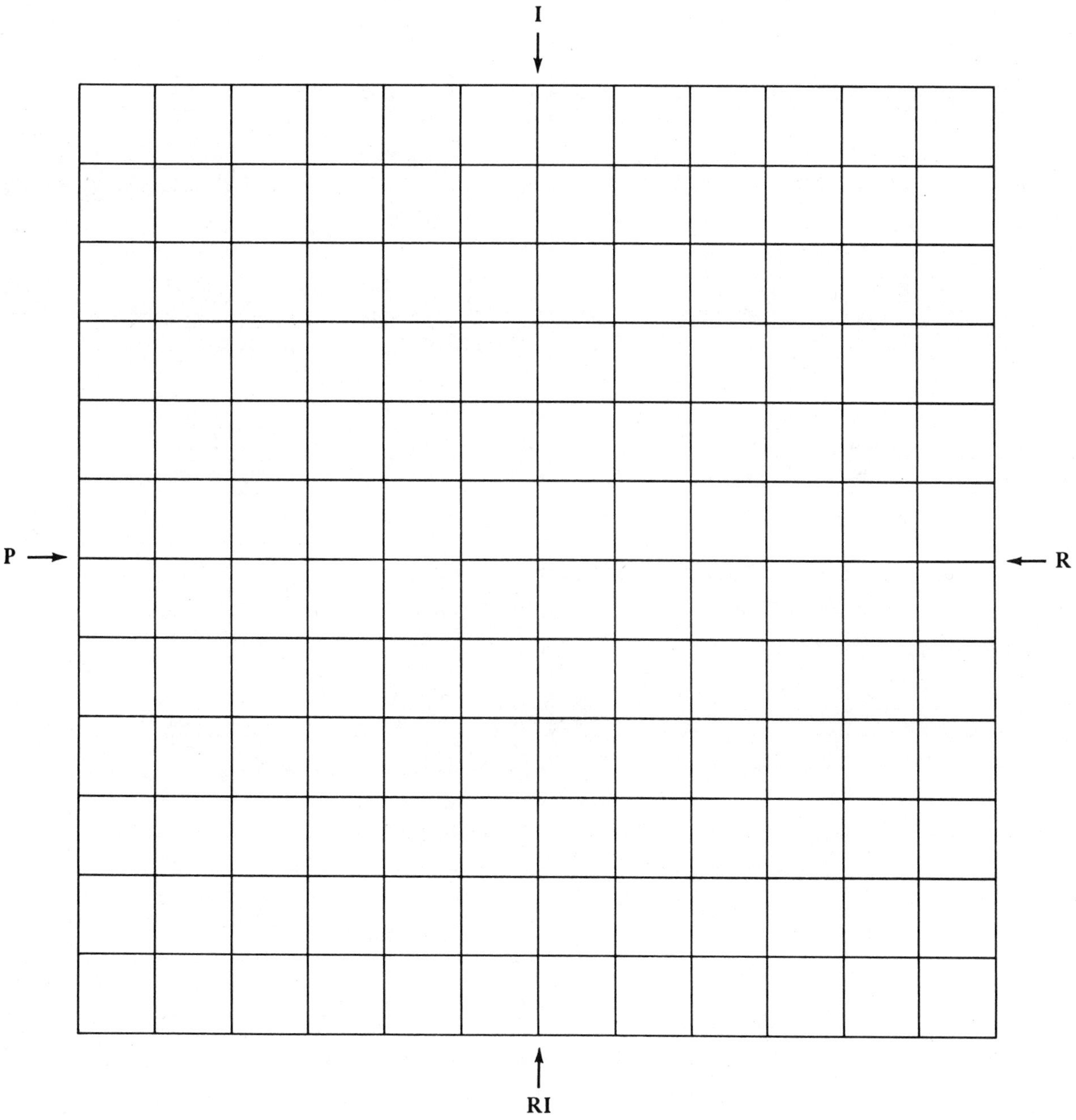

S. "The Moon Rises" is based upon the following set, in its prime zero form exclusively.

Trace the row throughout the music, using the numbering system indicated.

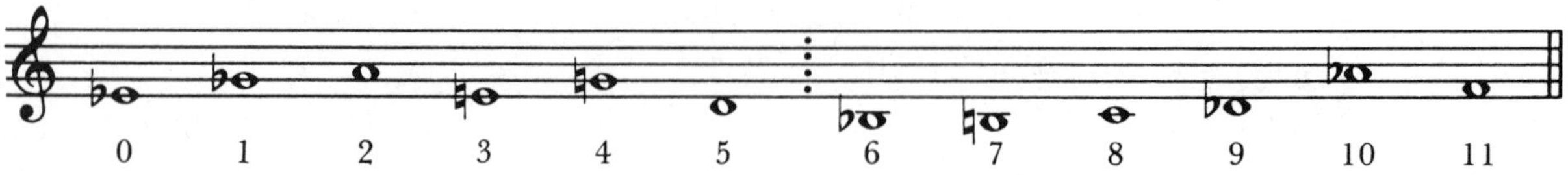

Křenek, "The Moon Rises," from *12 Short Piano Pieces Written in the Twelve-Tone Technique,* Op. 83

10
ppp
pp
p
15
8
p espr.
pp dolce
20

T. Using the row found in "The Moon Rises," compose a two-voice composition, the upper voice of which is based on prime zero, while the lower makes use of retrograde zero. You might wish to compose this for instruments other than piano, such as violin and cello or two flutes.

U. "Glass Figures," which follows, is based on the same row used in "The Moon Rises," but in its I^0 and R^0 forms. Write out these row forms on the staves provided:

P^0

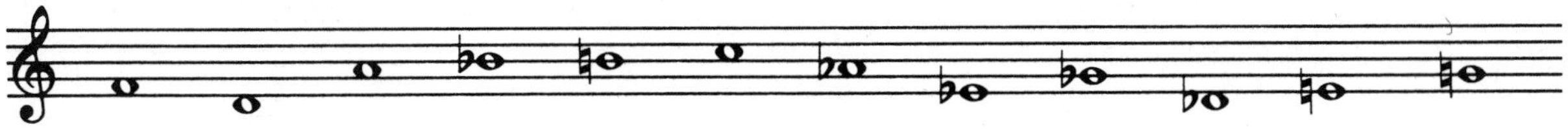

I^0

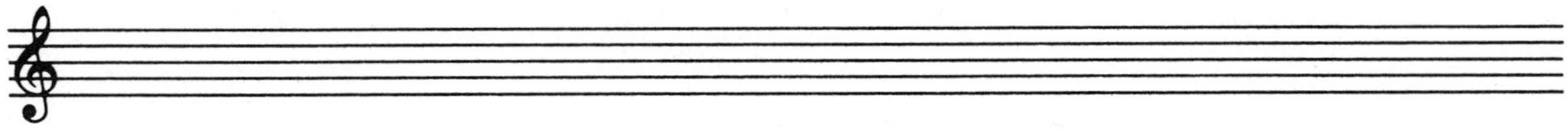

R^0

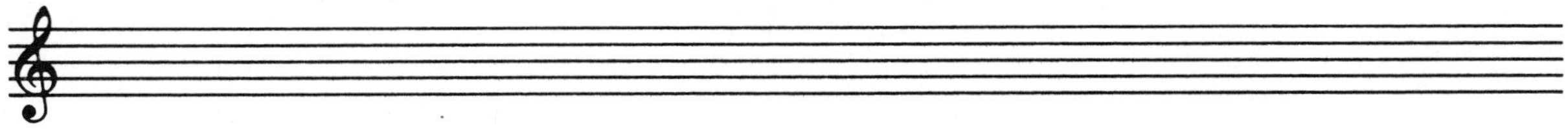

In examining the music, you will note that the first measure of the right hand opens with the first three pitches of I^0, while the left hand features the first two pitches of R^0. The third note of this latter set, D♭, is accommodated by the right hand, since the third pitch of I^0 is also a D♭. Following this, the roles of the set forms are reversed, with the left hand picking up I^0 while the right hand continues with R^0. Because of the frequency of this type of exchange where two or more row forms are involved, it is advisable to use different colored pencils to indicate different pitch collections in operation.

Křenek, "Glass Figures," from *12 Short Piano Pieces Written in the Twelve-Tone Technique,* Op. 83

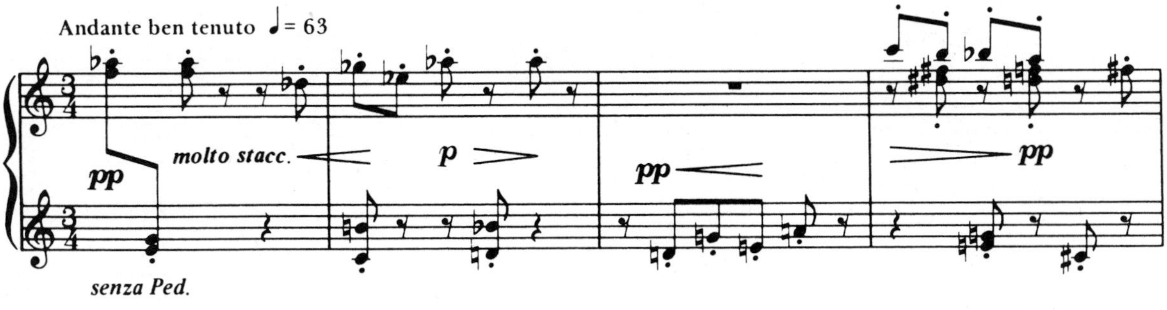

pp dolce legato
rit.
a tempo
pp
ppp
stacc.
pp espr. legato
mf
f
ff
f
mf
p
pp
pp
pp
ppp

V. Examine the setting of "Lo, How a Rose E'er Blooming" (first phrase) shown below. Discuss treatment of tonality and treatment of vertical sonorities.

Praetorius, "Lo, How a Rose E'er Blooming"

Experiment with varied settings of this or similar tunes. Your setting might feature tall chords, clusters, or even an atonal accompaniment. Be careful not to introduce too many textures; there should be some consistency of style.

W. Find scores and listen to recordings of works that illustrate the compositional principles mentioned in this chapter. Then try the following assignments:

1. Compose a short piece featuring aleatoric or indeterminate elements. Prepare a performance for class.
2. Analyze and write a summary of a piece that combines live and recorded music. Based upon your findings, compose a piece in this style.
3. Compose a piece featuring special effects for your instrument or voice. Perform the piece in class.
4. Select a three-note cell which will form the basis for a minimalist piece. Your composition should be based entirely upon permutations, transpositions, and rhythmic modifications of this cell. Experiment with various timbres and registers. Have the piece performed in class. Be sure that your performance directions are perfectly clear. (Hint: Your class performance will go much better if you arrange at least a brief rehearsal first!)